CAGLIARI TRAVEL GUIDE

Discover Cagliari's Top Attractions, Hidden Gems, Outdoor Activities, Culture & Local Secrets For Adventurous Solo Explorer

WILLELM H. VOLK

All rights reserved. No part of this publication may be reproduced, distributed, or transmitted in any form or by any means, including photocopying, recording, or other electronic or mechanical methods, without the prior written permission of the publisher, except in the case of brief quotations embodied in critical reviews and certain other noncommercial uses permitted by copyright law.

Copyright © 2025 by WILLELM H. VOLK

TABLE OF CONTENTS

Chapter 1: Introduction to Cagliari *12*
- Welcome to Cagliari: 13
- Why Visit Cagliari: 14
- Quick Facts: 15
- Getting Around Cagliari: 17
- When to Visit: 19
- Safety, Etiquette, and Traveler Tips 21
- Local Culture and Lifestyle: 22

Chapter 2: Top 10 Attractions in Cagliari *24*
- Castello District 24
- Bastione di Saint Remy 25
- Cattedrale di Santa Maria 26
- Roman Amphitheatre 28
- National Archaeological Museum 29
- Poetto Beach 31
- Torre dell'Elefante 32
- San Benedetto Market 33
- Botanical Garden of Cagliari 35
- Molentargius Natural Park 36

Chapter 3: Hidden Gems and Off-the-Beaten-Path *38*
- Sella del Diavolo Hike 38
- Villa di Tigellio 39
- Calamosca Beach 40
- Grotta della Vipera 42
- Monte Urpinu Park 43

Chiesa di Sant'Efisio	44
Museo d'Arte Siamese	45
Marina Piccola	47
Quartiere Villanova:	48
Is Mirrionis Street Art:	49

Chapter 4: Outdoor Adventures and Nature — *52*

Hiking the Devil's Saddle (Sella del Diavolo) Trail	52
Cycling Along Poetto's Coastal Path	53
Birdwatching at Molentargius Natural Park	54
Kayaking & Stand-Up Paddleboarding around Cagliari Bay	56
Snorkeling & Diving near Calamosca	57
Exploring Monte Urpinu's Forest Trails	58
Windsurfing & Sailing on the Gulf of Angels	60

Chapter 5: Food, Markets, and Gastronomy — *62*

Must-Try Sardinian Dishes in Cagliari	62
Where to Eat Like a Local:	63
Top Seafood Spots in the Marina District	65
San Benedetto Market:	67
Wine Bars and Regional Varietals	68
Best Gelaterias in the City	70
Street Food:	73

Chapter 6: Art, Music, and Cultural Life — *76*

Cagliari's Contemporary Art Spaces	76
Teatro Lirico di Cagliari	77
Sardinian Folk Festivals and Traditions	79
Local Craftsmanship:	81

- The Role of Sardinian Language in Culture — 83
- Live Music Venues and Jazz Bars — 84
- Cultural Centers and Creative Spaces — 86

Chapter 7: Beaches and Waterfront Escapes — 88
- Poetto Beach — 88
- Calamosca Beach — 89
- Mari Pintau — 90
- Spiaggia di Solanas — 91
- Punta Molentis — 93
- Spiaggia di Nora — 94
- Tuerredda Beach — 96

Chapter 8: Day Trips and Excursions from Cagliari — 98
- Nora Archaeological Park — 98
- Villasimius & Porto Giunco — 99
- Su Nuraxi di Barumini: — 101
- Pula Town & Workshops: — 102
- Iglesias & Mining Heritage — 103
- Costa Rei Beach — 105
- Barumini + Nora Combined Excursion — 106

Chapter 9: Shopping and Local Products — 108
- Via Manno and Via Garibaldi — 108
- Sardinian Jewelry and Coral Pieces — 109
- Local Food Souvenirs: — 111
- Traditional Handwoven Textiles and Rugs — 113
- Artisan Markets in Castello and Villanova — 114
- Bookstores, Art Shops, and Independent Makers — 116

Sustainable and Eco-Friendly Shopping in Cagliari _____ 118

Chapter 10: Practical Information and Travel Tips _____ *120*

How to Get to Cagliari: _____ 120

Navigating the City: _____ 121

Cost Breakdown: _____ 122

Language Tips: _____ 124

Health and Safety Tips for Travelers _____ 126

Internet, SIM Cards, and Staying Connected _____ 127

Accessibility and Traveling with Kids or Seniors _____ 129

Chapter 11: Suggested Itineraries for Every Type of Traveler _____ *132*

Cagliari in One Day: _____ 132

A Perfect Weekend: _____ 133

5-Day Itinerary: _____ 135

7-Day Deep Dive: _____ 137

Cagliari for Families: _____ 139

Cagliari for Food Lovers: _____ 140

Adventure & Nature Itinerary: _____ 142

Conclusion _____ *144*

DISCLAIMER

1. The prices provided are approximate and may vary due to factors such as personal choices, tour operators, or seasonal changes. It is recommended to confirm the latest prices and availability before making any travel plans.

2. You may notice that this guide does not include the usual array of photographs found in many travel books. You might be wondering, "Why not?" This choice reflects our commitment to sparking your imagination, inspiring curiosity, and immersing you in the spirit of Cagliari.

By excluding images, we encourage you to embrace the excitement of discovery. This decision isn't just about being different, it's about enhancing your experience. With vivid descriptions and detailed narratives, we aim to help you picture Cagliari's breathtaking landscapes, diverse wildlife, and rich cultural heritage. Our goal is to craft a journey that leaves a lasting impression, offering an experience that transcends the ordinary

SCAN CAGLIARI'S MAP BARCODE

Using the Barcode to Access Your Map

1. Download a QR Code Scanner app onto your mobile device from the Google Play Store.

2. Open the app and scan the barcode by selecting it.

3. Choose the browsing option that pops up, which will direct you to a new page displaying a map of Cagliari.

4. The map is now available and ready for use.

A NOTE TO OUR READERS

About This Guide's Organization

Dear Traveler,

As you use this guide, you may notice that some details appear in multiple sections. This is an intentional design to make your planning smoother and ensure essential information is always at your fingertips.

Why Key Details Are Repeated

Travel planning often doesn't follow a straightforward path. You might start with accommodation, switch to transportation options, and later revisit safety tips for specific areas. To align with this natural process, we've structured the guide so key information is accessible across all relevant sections.

For Example:

- Restaurant hours might be listed in both the "Dining Guide" and "Evening Activities" sections.
- Transportation options could appear in "Getting Around" as well as in attraction descriptions.
- Safety tips may be included in both the "Safety Guidelines" chapter and individual neighborhood profiles.

The Benefits of This Approach:

- Reduces the need for constant cross-referencing.
- Ensure critical information is easily accessible.
- Provides tailored, context-specific insights for each topic.
- Supports varied planning styles and preferences.
- Allows each chapter to work as a standalone resource.

How to Use This Guide Effectively:

- Explore sections in any order that suits your interests.
- Trust that important details will be repeated where relevant.
- Use the index to quickly find specific topics.
- Treat repeated information as helpful reinforcement of key details.

Our Promise to You

Our goal is to provide a guide that's practical, user-friendly, and efficient. By repeating essential details across relevant sections, we aim to minimize the need for page-turning, making your trip planning easier and more enjoyable.

Chapter 1: Introduction to Cagliari

Cagliari greets you with a warm sea breeze, sunlit streets, and a promise of discovery at every turn. You might have heard about Sardinia's pristine beaches or its ancient ruins, but Cagliari is so much more than a stopover—it's a place that weaves history and modern life into a tapestry you'll remember long after you've left.

I still recall my first evening in the Castello district, winding up narrow stone staircases as the sky turned pink. Up top, the city spread out before me—the red rooftops, the glint of the Poetto shoreline, and fishermen unloading their day's catch in Marina Piccola. That moment showed me how Cagliari marries its past and present: medieval walls stand guard over cafés where locals sip bitter espresso, and Roman amphitheaters sit quietly amid bustling neighborhoods.

This guide is here to help you feel Cagliari, not just see it. Want to taste the freshest ricci (sea urchin) straight from the Gulf of Angels? You'll learn exactly where to go—and when the fishermen bring in their boats at dawn. Curious about local life beyond the beaches? I'll share tips on wandering Villanova's colorful alleyways, where a friendly neighbor might invite you to join a midday card game over a glass of mirto. Practical advice, like catching the Number 1 bus from Piazza Yenne to Poetto Beach or finding the best time to tour the National Archaeological Museum without crowds, will save you time and help you dive deeper.

You won't find bland lists of "must-see" spots here. Instead, each chapter draws on real moments—like the surprise flamenco performance I stumbled upon in a tiny courtyard, or the way a sudden rain shower turned a routine market trip into an unexpected Sardinian dance lesson under a shared umbrella. These are the kinds of experiences that make Cagliari unforgettable, and they're what I want you to discover.

Throughout these pages, I've organized everything into easy-to-follow sections: top attractions, hidden gems, outdoor adventures, local eats, and more. Each section offers clear directions, honest cost estimates, and timing suggestions—whether it's arriving early to beat the midday heat at Sella del Diavolo or planning your visit to Nora around the golden-hour light for gorgeous photos. You'll also find practical tips on language ("grazie," "per favore," and a few Sardinian phrases that earn you a smile), safety pointers, and the best ways to connect—like grabbing a local SIM card at Elmas airport or hopping on a shared bike to explore the waterfront.

By the end of this guide, you'll have everything you need to craft your ideal Cagliari experience, whether that's a laid-back week of beach days and café visits, a whirlwind weekend of history and eats, or an active adventure hiking coastal trails and birdwatching in salt flats. Cagliari isn't just a place on the map—it's a feeling of sun, salt, and Sardinian spirit that stays with you. Ready to start? Let's go uncover the heart of Cagliari together.

Welcome to Cagliari:

Cagliari is the kind of place where you can slow down, breathe deeply, and feel like you've stepped into a different rhythm of life. This section introduces the spirit of the city and helps you understand what makes Cagliari such a special starting point for your Sardinian adventure.

Cagliari is the capital of Sardinia, one of Italy's most unique and autonomous regions. Sitting quietly on the island's southern coast, the city stretches from a gentle bay inland toward hills dotted with historic buildings. What makes Cagliari different from many other Italian cities is its easygoing charm. It doesn't shout for your attention—it draws you in slowly, with morning light on stone walls, the smell of baking bread, and sea air that never seems far away.

From your first walk through the old Castello district to your first plate of handmade pasta, you'll notice that things move at their own pace here. This is not a place overrun with mass tourism. Instead, locals go about their lives as they always have—shopping at open-air markets, enjoying evening strolls along Via Roma, and gathering with friends at simple cafés that haven't changed in decades.

Cagliari is also compact and easy to explore. You don't need to plan every detail. A short walk often leads to hidden viewpoints, small art galleries, or a quiet piazza where you can sit and people-watch. You might find yourself exploring ancient Roman ruins in the morning and relaxing at the beach in the afternoon—without ever needing to rush.

In many ways, this city gives you the best of both worlds: the rich culture and architecture of an Italian capital, mixed with the relaxed lifestyle of a coastal town. It's ideal for travelers who want to explore but don't want to feel overwhelmed.

Whether it's your first trip to Sardinia or your fifth time in Italy, Cagliari welcomes you with a warm smile and an open invitation to take things slow, enjoy the small moments, and let the city's simple beauty unfold naturally.

Why Visit Cagliari:

Cagliari may not be as famous as Rome or Venice, but it offers something many larger cities can't—a perfect mix of culture, sea, food, and authenticity. This section explains why this underrated city deserves a spot on your travel list.

One of the main reasons people fall in love with Cagliari is the balance it offers. You don't have to choose between a cultural trip and a beach vacation—here, you can have both in the same day. In the morning, you could walk through centuries-old fortifications and churches, and in the afternoon, you could be swimming in the clear waters of Poetto Beach.

The historic Castello district sits on a hill, offering wide views over the city and the sea. Its narrow streets and tall stone buildings hold centuries of history—from the days of Spanish rule to modern times. Walking through this neighborhood feels like stepping back in time, and it's one of the most photographed parts of the city for good reason.

For those interested in ancient history, the Roman Amphitheatre is a must-see. Carved directly into the hillside, it's a striking reminder of Cagliari's past. Nearby, the National Archaeological Museum showcases one of the most important collections of Sardinian artifacts, giving visitors insight into a civilization that predates the Roman Empire.

Food is another highlight of the city. Sardinian cuisine is both familiar and surprising. You'll recognize many Italian staples—fresh pasta, seafood, and cheese—but there's also a strong island identity in the flavors. One local favorite is **culurgiones**, a type of handmade stuffed pasta that resembles dumplings.

They're usually filled with potato, cheese, and mint, and served with a simple tomato sauce.

Seafood is everywhere in Cagliari, especially in the Marina district near the port. You'll find restaurants offering dishes like **fregola with clams**, grilled mullet, and **bottarga** (cured fish roe) sprinkled on pasta. Meals here are not rushed—they're social, often lasting two hours or more, and usually shared with local wine like **Cannonau** or **Vermentino**.

Nature is never far from reach. One of the most unique features near the city is **Molentargius Park**, a protected wetland where flamingos can be seen in the wild. Just a short bus or bike ride away from the center, it's a great place for walking, cycling, or birdwatching. The park is especially beautiful at sunrise and sunset, when the light reflects off the water and the birds are most active.

Then there are the neighborhoods that give Cagliari its soul. **Villanova** is a colorful and quiet area full of charm. The streets are lined with plants, murals, and local artisan shops. It's not uncommon to stumble upon a small workshop where someone is weaving textiles or carving wood by hand. This part of the city feels personal—like you're being shown someone's home, not just a tourist site.

For art lovers, Cagliari has several small but impressive galleries and cultural centers. These often focus on Sardinian artists or host temporary exhibitions that highlight the island's contemporary scene. The city's artistic identity blends traditional themes with modern interpretations, offering a deeper view of Sardinia's culture.

Finally, there's the atmosphere—relaxed, friendly, and welcoming. Locals are used to visitors but haven't grown tired of them. People are happy to help if you're lost, recommend a good restaurant, or share a bit of history if you show genuine interest. Even a simple coffee break can turn into a memorable exchange.

Quick Facts:

Before diving into the heart of Cagliari, it helps to understand the basic everyday things that make your stay smoother—from what language people speak to how to pay for a coffee or behave in a small local shop. These simple insights can make a big difference in how you're received and how easily you move around.

Language

The main language spoken in Cagliari is **Italian**, but it's not the only one. You may also hear **Sardinian**, a local language that has deep roots and a proud place in the island's identity. Sardinian (or "Sardu") is not just an accent—it's a completely different dialect, and it's still used, especially among older residents and in rural areas.

Most younger people and workers in the tourism sector speak at least some English, but not everyone does. It's useful to learn a few simple Italian phrases to show respect and help you get by:

- *Per favore* – Please
- *Grazie* – Thank you
- *Dov'è il bagno?* – Where is the bathroom?
- *Un caffè, per favore* – A coffee, please

Using even a few words of Italian often brings smiles and friendlier service. Locals appreciate visitors who make the effort, even if your pronunciation isn't perfect.

Currency

Cagliari, like the rest of Italy, uses the **euro (€)**. Credit and debit cards are widely accepted in hotels, restaurants, and larger stores. However, it's wise to **carry some cash**, especially if you plan to shop at open-air markets, stop by a small café, or visit less touristy neighborhoods where cards might not be accepted.

ATMs (known as **"bancomat"**) are easy to find in the city center, and most have English language options. Withdraw cash in reasonable amounts to avoid multiple bank fees if your card is from abroad.

When dining out or shopping, prices are usually marked clearly, and haggling is not a common practice in Sardinia—except maybe at some small flea markets where friendly bargaining may happen.

Local Customs

Sardinians are known for being warm, proud, and generous with their hospitality. Being polite and respectful is very important. It's customary to **greet people when entering a shop or café**. Saying "Buongiorno" (Good morning) or "Buonasera" (Good evening) is a simple but appreciated gesture.

Meal times are taken seriously and often enjoyed slowly. Lunch usually happens between **1:00 PM and 3:00 PM**, and dinner starts from **8:00 PM onwards**. Many small shops and restaurants **close for a few hours in the afternoon**—a sort of "siesta" that is still practiced widely. Use this time to relax, explore a quiet park, or enjoy a coffee.

Sardinians also place value on family, traditions, and community. Don't be surprised if you see large groups dining together well into the evening or hear traditional music during weekend street festivals.

Tipping

Tipping in Cagliari is **not expected**, but it is appreciated. Most restaurants include a small service charge (*coperto*) on the bill, but if you feel the service was good, leaving a few extra euros or rounding up is a kind gesture.

A good rule of thumb is:

- Leave **5–10%** in sit-down restaurants.
- In cafés and bars, rounding up to the nearest euro is fine.
- Taxis don't expect a tip, but you can round up to the next full euro if you wish.

Remember, a **friendly "thank you" or "grazie mille"** often means more than a tip.

Getting Around Cagliari:

Once you arrive in Cagliari, getting around is simple and often enjoyable. Whether you walk through the city's historic streets, hop on a bus, or rent a bike, the city offers several easy ways to explore.

Walking

Cagliari's city center is **very walkable**, especially around the main neighborhoods like **Castello**, **Marina**, **Stampace**, and **Villanova**. Most of the city's major landmarks, including the Cathedral, Bastione di Saint Remy, and the Roman Amphitheatre, are all within a **15- to 20-minute walking distance** from one another.

Comfortable walking shoes are a must, especially in older parts of town where streets are made of cobblestones and hills are common. The **Castello district**, in particular, sits on a hill, but the view from the top is worth the climb.

Street signs are clear, and Google Maps works well here. Don't hesitate to take your time and explore side alleys—you'll often discover hidden squares, colorful street art, or local bakeries with fresh pastries.

Public Buses

Cagliari has a **reliable and affordable bus network**, run by CTM (Compagnia Trasporti Municipali). A **single ticket costs €1.30** and is valid for 90 minutes. Tickets can be bought from **tobacco shops (tabacchi)**, vending machines, or via the **CTM BusFinder mobile app**.

The buses run frequently, especially between the **city center and Poetto Beach**, and they cover most parts of town, including connections to the airport and train station. Popular lines like **PF or PQ** go straight to the beachfront. Timetables are posted at most stops and available online.

Remember to validate your ticket when boarding the bus. Inspectors do random checks, and fines apply if your ticket isn't stamped.

Bikes and Scooters

If you enjoy cycling, you'll love the scenic ride along **Cagliari's seafront promenade**, especially early in the morning or at sunset. The bike path from the city center to Poetto Beach is flat and well-maintained, making it perfect for all skill levels.

You can rent bikes from several shops or use **bike-sharing services** available near Piazza Yenne and along Via Roma. Electric scooters are also available through various mobile apps.

Always follow the road signs and use the bike lanes where possible. Helmets are not required by law for adults but are recommended.

Taxis and Ride Apps

Taxis are easy to find in central areas and can also be booked by phone or via the **IT Taxi app**. They are safe and clean but more expensive than public transport. Most drivers speak basic English.

Cagliari doesn't have Uber or Bolt, so rely on licensed taxis. Use them for airport transfers, late-night returns, or when traveling with luggage. Fares are metered, and tipping is optional.

When to Visit:

Knowing when to go can make a big difference in how you experience Cagliari. The city offers something special in every season, from sunny beaches in the summer to quiet cultural walks in the winter. This section will help you decide what time of year fits your interests and expectations.

Spring (April to June)

Spring is one of the best times to visit Cagliari. The weather is mild, with temperatures ranging from 18 to 24°C (64–75°F). Flowers bloom across the city, especially in parks like Monte Urpinu and the Botanical Garden, creating colorful and fragrant surroundings. It's a great time for walking tours, hiking trails like the **Sella del Diavolo (Devil's Saddle)**, or simply enjoying a long lunch outdoors.

Spring also brings a special energy to the city thanks to **local festivals and religious celebrations**. The most famous is **Festa di Sant'Efisio**, held on **May 1st**, where thousands of people, many in traditional dress, join a long procession from the city to the nearby town of Nora. It's one of the most important and beautiful events in Sardinia. Hotels can get busy around this time, so booking early is a good idea if you plan to attend.

Summer (July to August)

Summer is peak tourist season in Cagliari. The days are hot, with temperatures often between 25 and 32°C (77–89°F). This is beach season, and places like **Poetto**

Beach fill with locals and visitors alike. If you enjoy sunbathing, swimming, and lively beach bars, this is the time to come.

Expect a lot of activity—live music, outdoor markets, open-air film nights, and busy restaurants. Make reservations ahead of time, especially for dinner in popular spots near the Marina or Castello. Boat tours to nearby coves and snorkeling spots also tend to book up fast, so plan at least a few days in advance.

The heat can be intense in the afternoons, so it's smart to take a long lunch or rest during the hottest part of the day. Most museums and indoor attractions stay open with air-conditioning, offering a break from the sun.

Autumn (September to October)

Autumn is a great time to visit if you want a calmer version of summer. The sea remains warm enough for swimming, and the crowds start to thin out. Daytime temperatures usually range from 22 to 28°C (72-82°F), which is perfect for exploring on foot without overheating.

This season also marks the beginning of **grape harvests** and **wine festivals** in Sardinia. While many vineyards are outside of Cagliari, you can often join half-day trips from the city to taste local wines like **Cannonau** and **Vermentino**. If you enjoy food and wine, this is a wonderful time to explore local flavors.

Accommodation prices tend to drop slightly after August, and it's easier to get tables at good restaurants without booking far in advance.

Winter (November to March)

Winter in Cagliari is cool but far from freezing. Expect temperatures between 10 and 16°C (50-61°F). There might be some rain, but many days are still sunny and mild compared to other parts of Europe.

This is **low season**, which means lower prices, quieter streets, and fewer tourists. It's an excellent time to visit if you prefer cultural sites over beach days. The **National Archaeological Museum, Roman Amphitheatre**, and **local art galleries** are open year-round and rarely crowded in winter.

Shops and restaurants remain open, although some beach kiosks and seasonal attractions may close for the season. Bring a jacket and maybe an umbrella, but don't let the cooler weather stop you—winter is the best time to experience the city like a local.

Safety, Etiquette, and Traveler Tips

Cagliari is a safe and welcoming place, but knowing a few simple tips will help you avoid problems and feel more comfortable. This section shares important details on how to stay safe, how to behave in public places, and a few things that will help you blend in with local customs.

General Safety

Cagliari is considered very safe for travelers. Violent crime is rare, and locals are generally helpful. That said, petty theft, like pickpocketing, can happen in crowded areas such as markets, public buses, and major attractions. Keep your bags zipped, don't flash valuables, and be aware of your surroundings.

At night, the city center is usually lively and well-lit. Still, avoid walking alone in poorly lit or unfamiliar neighborhoods after midnight, especially if you're carrying expensive gear or large amounts of cash.

Dining Tips

Many of the smaller trattorias and family-run restaurants change their menus daily, especially if they serve fresh fish. Don't be surprised if the waiter recites the day's options instead of giving you a printed menu. It's perfectly fine to ask for clarification or even request a translated explanation.

Tipping is not expected in most places. However, rounding up the bill or leaving a euro or two is always appreciated. In upscale restaurants, 5–10% is enough.

Dress Code

Cagliari is relaxed when it comes to dress. Shorts and t-shirts are fine in most settings. However, if you plan to visit churches or religious sites, cover your shoulders and wear knee-length clothing. You don't need formal clothes unless you're attending a special performance or fine dining venue.

Smoking Norms

Smoking is still fairly common in Italy. Many locals smoke outside cafes, at beach bars, or even on the sidewalk. If you prefer to avoid smoke, look for seating inside or check with the waiter for a non-smoking area.

Siesta Hours

Like many places in southern Europe, Cagliari observes a midday break. From about **1 PM to 4 PM**, many smaller shops and local businesses close. Supermarkets and larger chains usually stay open. Use this time to relax with lunch at a slow-paced café, visit a museum, or enjoy a nap like the locals do.

Local Etiquette

It's customary to greet people when entering small shops with a **"Buongiorno"** (good morning) or **"Buonasera"** (good evening). Locals appreciate polite manners and may be more willing to help if you make a friendly effort.

Try to avoid being loud in public places or while riding buses—quiet conversation is the norm. If someone helps you with directions or service, a warm "Grazie mille" (thank you very much) goes a long way.

Local Culture and Lifestyle:

To really understand Cagliari, you need to look beyond its beaches and historic buildings. The heart of the city lies in its people, their traditions, and the everyday way of life. Sardinians are known for their deep connection to family, food, and land. In this section, we'll explore what daily life feels like in Cagliari and how visitors can respectfully enjoy and be part of it.

Sardinian Pride in Identity

Sardinians are proud to be both Italian and distinctly Sardinian. The island has its own language, music, customs, and festivals that have been passed down through generations. You'll often hear the Sardinian language spoken between locals, especially older residents. While everyone understands Italian, hearing Sardinian used in shops, markets, and public spaces shows how strongly people here hold onto their roots.

Music, Art, and Daily Life
Music is an important part of local life. You may come across performances featuring the *launeddas*—an ancient wind instrument made from reeds. These traditional sounds are sometimes mixed with modern music, especially during local festivals or street celebrations. Street art is also a part of Cagliari's visual culture, especially in neighborhoods like Villanova and Is Mirrionis. Painted walls, handmade crafts, and colorful mosaics show how creativity plays a role in everyday expression.

Slow Living and Meal Culture
Daily life in Cagliari runs at a slower pace than in larger cities. Most people enjoy long meals with family or friends, and restaurants never rush guests to leave. Lunch is usually the biggest meal of the day and can last up to two hours. Dinner starts later in the evening, often around 8 PM or later. Eating is more than just food—it's a time to connect, talk, and relax.

Hospitality and Social Customs
If you get invited to someone's home, it's a big sign of trust and kindness. Bring a small gift—something like a bottle of local wine or a piece of regional cheese is thoughtful and appreciated. Locals are often curious and friendly toward visitors, especially those who show respect and interest in Sardinian culture.

Final Tip:
The concept of *"su connottu"*—which means "what is known and familiar"—describes how locals welcome others as if they're already part of the community. Show openness and appreciation, and you'll feel more like a guest of honor than just a tourist passing through.

Chapter 2: Top 10 Attractions in Cagliari

Castello District

The Castello District is where Cagliari began. Perched on a hill above the city, this ancient neighborhood holds centuries of history, charm, and Sardinian identity. Walking through its narrow streets feels like you've stepped into a storybook. It's not just a historic area—it's a living, breathing part of the city, where locals still hang laundry from balconies, sip espresso in quiet courtyards, and greet neighbors by name.

Address: Via Santa Croce, 09124 Cagliari
Price: Free
Activities: Explore the medieval lanes, discover churches and towers, shop for local crafts
How to Get There: From *Piazza Yenne*, it's a steep 10-minute walk uphill, or you can take buses 2 or 4 to the "Castello" stop.

Why You Should Visit:
Castello is more than a tourist stop—it's a place where everyday life and ancient architecture blend naturally. You'll find striking city views at almost every corner, including viewpoints like the Bastione and Via Santa Croce. Castello is also home to some of Cagliari's most important sites: the **Cattedrale di Santa Maria**, the **Torre dell'Elefante**, and the **National Archaeological Museum**.

But the real magic is in the atmosphere. The streets are cobbled and often narrow, lined with old stone buildings and little cafés tucked into corners. You'll see students heading to the University of Cagliari, shopkeepers opening shutters, and locals chatting in Sardinian dialect.

Best Time to Visit:
Early mornings (between 8 and 10 AM) are best, especially in summer. The

temperature is cooler, the streets are quieter, and the soft light makes for perfect photos.

Additional Info & Personal Anecdote:
One morning while exploring on my own, I turned into an alley and stumbled upon a tiny cork workshop. The owner, a friendly older man named Giorgio, was shaping pieces of cork bark into shoes. When he saw my interest, he offered to show me how it's done and even let me carve a piece myself. I walked away with a handmade cork keychain and a story I'll always remember. This is the kind of surprise that Castello offers—you never know what you'll find around the next corner.

Practical Tip: Wear comfortable shoes. The streets here can be uneven and steep in places. Also, bring a refillable water bottle—there are a few public fountains where you can top up.

Bastione di Saint Remy

If you're looking for a perfect spot to get your first wide-angle view of Cagliari, the **Bastione di Saint Remy** is where to go. Built in the 19th century on top of older fortifications, this grand staircase and terrace is one of the city's most recognizable landmarks. It connects the lower city with the upper Castello district and offers unbeatable panoramic views.

Address: Piazza Costituzione, 09124 Cagliari
Price: Free
Activities: Climb the stairs, enjoy views, relax on the terrace, attend events in summer
How to Get There: From *Largo Carlo Felice*, walk uphill toward *Piazza Costituzione*—you'll see the grand marble staircase straight ahead.

Why You Should Visit:
The Bastione is a mix of historical architecture and local life. It was originally built as a defensive structure but was redesigned into a more public space in the late 1800s. The *Passeggiata Coperta* (covered walkway) below the terrace sometimes hosts exhibitions and cultural events. But most visitors come for the

upper terrace, which gives a full 360-degree view of the city, port, and hills beyond.

Locals gather here at all times of day—especially at sunset. You'll see people sitting on the steps with gelato, artists sketching, couples taking selfies, and sometimes even street performers or musicians. The vibe is laid-back but lively.

Best Time to Visit:
Evening, just before sunset, is ideal. The light turns golden, and the view of the sun dipping below the horizon is spectacular. In summer, it's also cooler and more pleasant.

Additional Info & Personal Anecdote:
If you're lucky enough to visit during **Ferragosto** (around August 15th), you might catch a local jazz trio performing on the terrace. I once joined a group of locals dancing in a spontaneous circle—someone passed around cups of *Vermentino* (a crisp local white wine), and a young girl even started singing along. It felt like one of those moments where you're not just a tourist—you're part of something.

Practical Tip: There are benches on the terrace where you can sit and rest. Bring a snack or drink, especially in the evening. Also, keep an eye on local event posters—you might catch a photography exhibit or food tasting in the covered gallery space below.

Cattedrale di Santa Maria

In the heart of Cagliari's historic Castello district stands one of the city's most important landmarks: the Cattedrale di Santa Maria. It's more than just a place of worship—it's a living monument that showcases the island's layered history through its architecture and atmosphere.

Address: Piazza Palazzo, 09124 Cagliari
Price: Free (donations welcome)
Activities: Explore the main nave, view the chapels, climb the bell tower
How to get there: Located in Castello, just a 2-minute walk from Torre dell'Elefante
Best time to visit: Late morning (around 10–11 AM) to catch the light coming

through the stained-glass windows

Why visit: To experience centuries of Sardinian history carved into stone and marble

Detailed Description:
The Cattedrale di Santa Maria was originally built in the 13th century by the Pisans, and like many churches in Sardinia, it has gone through various renovations. As a result, what you see today is a fascinating mix of architectural styles—from Romanesque and Gothic to Baroque.

Walking up to the cathedral, you'll immediately notice its grand facade. It was rebuilt in the 1930s in a neo-Romanesque style, inspired by the churches of Pisa. Inside, the building opens into a cool, calm space with tall ceilings, marble floors, and a central nave lined with ornate chapels.

Don't miss the **Chapel of the Martyrs** in the crypt. This section holds the remains of over 170 martyrs discovered in the local catacombs. The space is small but atmospheric, with rows of niches and quiet corners perfect for a reflective moment.

If you're up for a bit of a climb, you can also visit the bell tower. It doesn't cost anything extra, and the views over Castello's rooftops and the Gulf of Cagliari are well worth the effort.

Anecdote:
I visited on a quiet November morning, not realizing it was the feast day of **Saint Cecilia**, the patron saint of music. To my surprise, a full choir was rehearsing in the main nave. The acoustics of the cathedral made their singing echo beautifully throughout the building. I remember sitting there for nearly half an hour, just listening, even though I hadn't planned to stay that long. It felt like being part of something deeply meaningful—even as a visitor.

Practical Tips:
- Dress modestly if you plan to enter (no sleeveless tops or short shorts)
- Flash photography isn't allowed inside
- Combine your visit with the nearby **Palazzo Regio** and **Torre dell'Elefante** for a full Castello experience

Whether you're into history, art, or just quiet moments in stunning surroundings, the Cattedrale di Santa Maria is a must-see in Cagliari.

Roman Amphitheatre

Tucked into a hillside just west of the city center, the **Roman Amphitheatre** of Cagliari is a powerful reminder of the island's role in ancient Roman life. This large, open-air structure is one of the most important archaeological sites in southern Sardinia and offers a glimpse into public entertainment almost 2,000 years ago.

Address: Via Sant'Ignazio, 09124 Cagliari
Price: €6 adults, €4 reduced (students, seniors)
Activities: Explore the seating areas, stand in the arena, check out underground passages
How to get there: Take bus 1 or 3 and get off at "SS 554/Sant'Ignazio," then walk for 3 minutes
Best time to visit: Early afternoon—tour groups usually come in the morning
Why visit: It's one of the largest Roman arenas outside of mainland Italy, and you can walk through it at your own pace

Detailed Description:
Dating back to the **2nd century AD**, the Roman Amphitheatre was carved directly into the limestone hill, which makes it unique compared to many free-standing arenas. At its peak, it could seat up to 10,000 spectators—quite impressive considering Cagliari's size at the time.

The site is fairly open, so wear sun protection if visiting on a hot day. There are stone steps leading up and down the seating tiers, giving you the chance to imagine where the local population once gathered to watch **gladiator fights, wild animal hunts, and public executions**.

While some of the structure was dismantled in the 19th century (stones were taken to build other parts of the city), much of it remains intact. You can walk through the **backstage areas** where animals and performers were kept before entering the arena.

Interpretive signs around the site explain the amphitheatre's history and significance. There's also a small ticket office where you can ask about **upcoming events**, as the space is sometimes used for concerts and plays during the summer.

Anecdote:
On one of my visits, I happened to see a local theater group rehearsing Shakespeare's *Julius Caesar*. They weren't even charging an audience—just practicing. I sat on a warm stone seat with a bottle of water and watched the scene unfold under the open sky. The play, the stone steps, and the historical setting all blended together in a surreal way. It was one of the most unexpected highlights of my trip.

Practical Tips:
- The terrain is uneven, so wear sturdy shoes
- There are no shaded areas inside—bring a hat or umbrella
- Not all areas are wheelchair accessible, but there are viewing spots near the entrance

Nearby Add-Ons:
After visiting the amphitheatre, head to the **Botanical Garden of Cagliari**, which is right next door. It makes a great contrast: ancient ruins followed by lush greenery and peace.

The Roman Amphitheatre might not be as famous as the Colosseum in Rome, but its quiet atmosphere and setting in a residential neighborhood give it a more personal, less touristy feel. It's ideal for those who enjoy exploring history up close and at their own pace.

National Archaeological Museum

If you're interested in ancient history and want to understand the deep cultural roots of Sardinia, the **National Archaeological Museum of Cagliari** is the place to visit. This museum is not only informative but also visually fascinating, offering a journey through 4,000 years of the island's past. From prehistoric relics to

Roman-era treasures, the exhibits help bring Sardinia's rich and often overlooked history to life.

Address: Via Santa Croce, 09124 Cagliari
Price: €8 for adults; free for those under 18
Activities: View ancient artifacts, read about Sardinian civilizations, see intricate Nuragic bronzes and Phoenician jewelry
How to get there: A short 7-minute downhill walk from the Castello district via Via Corte d'Appello
Best time to visit: Weekday mornings are ideal to avoid crowds and school tours

The museum is part of the **Cittadella dei Musei** complex and is well-organized, with bilingual signs in Italian and English. The exhibits are arranged chronologically, starting from the **Neolithic period** and moving through to the **Phoenician**, **Punic**, and **Roman** eras. The most iconic displays are the **Nuragic bronzes**—small metal statues made by Sardinia's mysterious Bronze Age civilization. Some of these bronzes represent warriors, archers, and animals and show surprising craftsmanship given their age.

You'll also find **Phoenician amulets**, **Egyptian scarabs**, **Roman mosaics**, and even early tools and weapons made from obsidian. For those unfamiliar with Sardinia's unique past, this museum is a crash course in everything from ancient trade networks to burial rituals.

A personal highlight for me was spotting a **tiny gold earring shaped like a ram**, placed in a simple display case. It looked so modern and detailed that at first, I thought it was a replica. But it was real—delicate, centuries old, and perfectly preserved. It's these small objects that help connect you to the people who lived on the island long before written records.

One useful tip: if you're traveling with children or are not a huge fan of reading museum panels, there's a free audio guide available through a QR code at the entrance. It makes the experience more interactive and helps explain the exhibits in a simple way.

For a better visit, avoid weekends or school holidays when the museum is busier. Photography without flash is allowed, and there are lockers for bags near the entrance.

Why visit? Because it offers the best introduction to Sardinia's ancient world— one that you won't find in beach brochures or tourist posters. It's a quiet, cool, and thoughtful stop where history comes alive in the most unexpected ways.

Poetto Beach

No visit to Cagliari would be complete without spending time at **Poetto Beach**. Stretching over eight kilometers, this wide sandy beach is one of the longest in Italy and is loved by locals and visitors alike. It offers a break from sightseeing and is great for swimming, relaxing, or enjoying a simple meal by the sea.

Address: Lungomare Poetto, 09126 Cagliari
Price: Free entry; sunbeds and umbrellas available from around €5
Activities: Swimming, sunbathing, beach volleyball, walking or cycling the promenade, eating at seafront cafés
How to get there: Take bus lines 1 or 5 from Piazza Matteotti; it's about a 20-minute ride
Best time to visit: May to June for warm weather and fewer crowds

The beach is popular for good reason. The sand is soft and pale, the water is clear with a shallow drop-off—perfect for kids and casual swimmers—and there are plenty of services available. You can rent a sunbed and umbrella, join a morning yoga class, or simply walk the promenade and enjoy the sea breeze.

There's also a long cycling and jogging path that runs parallel to the beach, making it a favorite among active locals. Along the beach, you'll find **"chioschi"**, or beach kiosks, where you can grab coffee, pizza, ice cream, or cocktails, depending on the time of day.

What makes Poetto stand out is that it feels natural and easygoing, not overly touristy. On weekdays, you'll see Sardinian families, teenagers playing volleyball, and older locals having a morning swim. On weekends in summer, it can get crowded, especially in the central sections. For a quieter experience, head to the **eastern end** near **Marina Piccola**, where the crowds thin and the views of the **Sella del Diavolo** (Devil's Saddle) are stunning.

A personal story: One Saturday morning, I joined a local fitness group for a **beach bootcamp**. We met just after sunrise, did stretches facing the water, jogged along the shore, and even used driftwood for light strength training. Afterward, someone suggested a gelato stop nearby—and it turned out to be one of the best pistachio scoops I've ever had.

For practical advice, bring a hat, sunscreen, and water bottle if you're visiting midday. There are **public toilets and showers** spaced out along the beach, and buses run frequently back into town. If you're renting a car, parking is available but can fill up fast during peak summer.

Why visit? Poetto offers more than just sun and sand. It's a piece of daily life in Cagliari, where you can relax like a local, enjoy nature, and recharge in one of the most beautiful urban beaches in the Mediterranean.

Torre dell'Elefante

Step into the Middle Ages by visiting one of Cagliari's most iconic and enduring landmarks. Torre dell'Elefante (Tower of the Elephant) is a medieval watchtower built in 1307 during the rule of the Pisan Republic. This massive stone structure was part of the city's defense system and today remains one of the few places where you can physically touch and experience the city's medieval history.

Address: Piazza Arsenale, 09124 Cagliari
Entry Fee: €4 (includes access to the nearby Torre di San Pancrazio)
Activities: Climbing the narrow steps, viewing the elephant carving, reading medieval inscriptions, taking in panoramic views
How to Get There: Located inside the Castello district. If you're starting from Piazza Yenne, it's a 10-minute walk uphill or a short bus ride (Bus 8 or 10) to Piazza Arsenale.
Best Time to Visit: Mid-morning or late afternoon when the sunlight casts shadows that make the stone carvings stand out.

Why You Should Visit:
This tower is not just a great spot for a panoramic view—it's a real piece of Sardinia's medieval history. The structure is made of white limestone, with three

massive stone walls and one open side with wooden platforms and stairways. It was designed to defend the Castello area from attacks and has withstood centuries of battles, sieges, and political changes. The elephant-shaped sculpture, located on one side of the tower, gave it its name and has become a local symbol.

Climbing to the top can feel a bit intense—the stairs are steep and narrow—but it's worth the effort. At the summit, you'll be rewarded with one of the best views of the city, stretching over rooftops, the harbor, and the distant mountains.

Additional Info & Anecdote:
When I visited, I was struck by how quiet it was inside despite being in the city center. The stones absorb sound, giving the place a hushed, almost sacred feeling. What fascinated me most, though, was the graffiti carved into the stone by prisoners from centuries ago—some were curses aimed at governors, others were names and dates. One of them read something like, "Here I suffer but my words remain." That stayed with me. It made the tower feel human, not just historic.

If you're visiting with children or anyone afraid of heights, take care on the stairs—there are rails, but the climb is open on one side. Wear comfortable shoes, bring a water bottle, and allow about 45 minutes for the visit.

San Benedetto Market

San Benedetto Market isn't just a place to shop—it's a way to understand Sardinia through its flavors and people. Located right in the heart of Cagliari, this massive indoor market is a daily stop for locals looking for fresh ingredients, and a must-visit for travelers who want to experience the real food culture of the island.

Address: Via Francesco Cocco Ortu (not Piazza Yenne), 09128 Cagliari
Price: Entry is free. Many food samples and street bites cost between €1–€5.
Activities: Tasting local cheeses and seafood, buying spices and produce, chatting with vendors, photography
How to Get There: A 5-minute walk from Largo Carlo Felice, or take bus lines 1 or M (Metro Cagliari) to the "Mercato di San Benedetto" stop.

Best Time to Visit: Between 8:00 AM and 11:00 AM. After 12:30 PM, many vendors begin packing up.

Why You Should Visit:

This market has two floors and covers over 8,000 square meters, making it one of the largest covered markets in Europe. The ground floor is packed with fresh fish and seafood—octopus, mussels, shrimp, tuna steaks—while the upper floor is where you'll find meats, cheeses, vegetables, fruit, bread, pastries, and local delicacies.

If you're new to Sardinian food, look out for *bottarga* (cured fish roe), *pecorino sardo* (local sheep's cheese), *pane carasau* (crisp flatbread), and *mirto* (a myrtle berry liqueur). Many vendors will let you try a small piece of cheese or slice of sausage if you ask politely in Italian or just gesture with a smile.

It's not just about food—it's also about the experience. You'll see elderly men debating over which tomatoes are best for sauce, women with shopping trolleys comparing cuts of meat, and young chefs picking herbs for their daily menu. It's a lively, colorful, and very real part of Cagliari.

Additional Info & Anecdote:

During my visit, I stopped at a seafood stall and asked the vendor how to cook sardines. He didn't just give me a recipe—he took a few sardines out, showed me how to gut and season them, and told me to try grilling them with a squeeze of lemon and a pinch of salt. I went home and followed his advice—it was simple, but incredibly tasty.

Another highlight was the cheese section upstairs. I found a soft cheese infused with saffron, something I'd never tried before. The vendor explained that saffron is grown in Sardinia and often used in festive dishes. Moments like this—where food becomes a story—are what make San Benedetto Market so special.

If you're planning to cook during your stay in Cagliari, this is the perfect place to stock up. And even if you're not, it's a fun spot to wander through, take photos, and grab a quick snack. There are bakeries on-site where you can get freshly made pastries, and coffee bars for a strong espresso and a sweet *sebadas* (fried pastry with honey and cheese).

Tips:

- Bring cash; many vendors don't accept cards.
- Don't touch produce unless invited—point or ask.
- It gets busy on Saturdays; weekdays are calmer.
- Bring your own shopping bag or tote.

Botanical Garden of Cagliari

Sometimes the best way to understand a city is to take a quiet walk through its green spaces. Tucked behind the bustling Castello district and next to the National Archaeological Museum, the **Botanical Garden of Cagliari (Orto Botanico di Cagliari)** is a calm, natural retreat that brings a different side of the city to life. Whether you're a plant lover or just looking for a place to rest your feet, this garden offers a peaceful break from museums and monuments.

Address: Via Sant'Ignazio da Laconi, 09124 Cagliari
Entry Price: €3 for adults, €1 for visitors under 18
How to Get There: Walk down Via Santa Croce from Castello or reach it directly from the Archaeological Museum—only a short 2-minute walk
Best Time to Visit: Spring (March to May) is ideal. This is when the gardens are bursting with color, and the air is fresh and fragrant.

The garden covers around five hectares and was first opened in 1866. Today, it is home to more than 2,000 plant species, many of which are native to Sardinia or the Mediterranean region. You'll also find tropical and desert plants brought in from Africa, Australia, and the Americas.

As you walk through the garden, you'll notice clearly marked paths that guide you through different plant zones—each labeled for easy identification. The Mediterranean section is full of familiar plants like olive trees, rosemary, and myrtle, while the desert zone features a towering collection of cacti and succulents. There's also a tropical greenhouse with rare species, although it's not always open to the public.

One of the best spots in the garden is the pond area, where water lilies float gently, and frogs occasionally croak in the background. Wooden benches are scattered throughout the garden, inviting you to sit down, read a book, or just enjoy a moment of stillness.

Why visit? Because it's a refreshing change of pace. The garden is never too crowded, even during peak season, making it a perfect place for travelers who need a break from sightseeing. It's also a great family spot—kids can roam freely, and there's enough shade to stay comfortable on warmer days.

Personal anecdote: On one of my visits, I noticed a local artist quietly sketching the cactus garden, deeply focused on capturing the shadows between the spines. We exchanged a few words about how peaceful the place was, and he said, "This is where I come to clear my head." That moment summed up the feel of the garden—simple, reflective, and quietly inspiring.

Additional Tip: Wear comfortable shoes, especially if you plan to walk slowly through the entire site. While there are shaded areas, bring water with you during warmer months. The garden closes around sunset, so it's best to go earlier in the day.

Molentargius Natural Park

Nature lovers and birdwatchers will find something truly special at Molentargius Natural Park. Located just a few minutes from the city center, this park is one of the few places in Europe where you can see pink flamingos living in the wild—right next to an urban setting. It's a rare mix of nature, history, and sustainability all rolled into one visit.

Address: Viale dei Giudicati, 09126 Cagliari
Entry Price: Free (bike rental available from €4/hr)
How to Get There: Take Bus 7 or 20 and get off at the "Molentargius" stop; from there, it's a short walk to the park entrance
Best Time to Visit: Late afternoon, especially in spring and early summer, when flamingos gather in large numbers near the water

The park was once an active salt production site, and the name *Molentargius* comes from the Sardinian word for "donkey driver," referring to workers who used donkeys to move salt. Today, the salt flats are no longer in commercial use, but they remain an important ecological habitat.

Flamingos are the stars of the show. These elegant birds, with their pink feathers and slow, graceful movements, can often be seen standing in shallow waters. You can spot them from designated viewing platforms or along the many cycling and walking paths that wind through the park.

There's also a **small salt museum** inside the park that explains how the salt pans operated and how the area was transformed into a protected reserve. Entry to the museum is usually free, and it only takes about 15-20 minutes to explore.

One of the most enjoyable ways to experience the park is by bike. There's an information kiosk near the main entrance that offers bike rentals starting at around €4 per hour. The trails are flat and easy to navigate, even for beginners or families with kids. If you'd rather walk, there are shaded routes that take you past lagoons, marshes, and even old industrial buildings reclaimed by nature.

Why visit? This park shows a different side of Cagliari—one where nature and city coexist beautifully. It's peaceful, open, and unique in its combination of wildlife, wetlands, and industrial history.

Personal anecdote: I rented a bike and slowly pedaled past reed beds and salt pools, stopping often to watch birds take flight. At one point, I rounded a corner and was suddenly surrounded by flamingos on both sides—dozens of them standing like pink statues, their reflections glowing in the afternoon light. It was one of the most unexpectedly beautiful scenes I've come across while traveling.

Extra Tips: Bring binoculars if you're into birdwatching. Pack water and sunscreen, as there's little shade on many of the open trails. The park is large, so allow at least 2-3 hours if you want to explore thoroughly.

Chapter 3: Hidden Gems and Off-the-Beaten-Path

Sella del Diavolo Hike

A scenic hike just minutes from the city, Sella del Diavolo offers nature lovers a peaceful escape with breathtaking views. It's one of those places that locals often enjoy, while many visitors miss it altogether. If you enjoy hiking or photography, this is a perfect way to see another side of Cagliari.

Address: Trailhead at Via Roma, near Calamosca Beach
Price: Free
Activities: Coastal hiking, panoramic viewpoints, nature photography
How to Get There: Take Bus #5 from Piazza Matteotti (city center) and get off at the "Calamosca" stop. From there, it's about a 10-minute uphill walk to the trailhead.
Best Time to Visit: Early morning (7:00-9:00 AM) in spring or autumn is ideal. Temperatures are cooler, and you might catch a beautiful sunrise.
Why You Should Visit: This spot gives you one of the best views in all of Cagliari. The Gulf of Angels stretches out below you, and on clear days, you can see all the way to Capo Carbonara.

What to Expect:
The trail begins gently, winding its way through Mediterranean shrubs and wildflowers. It's not a very difficult hike, but some parts are rocky and uneven. You'll want to wear proper shoes—flip-flops are a bad idea here. As you climb higher, the sea comes into view on both sides, with cliffs, boats, and salt flats creating a beautiful contrast of colors.

The hike takes around 45 minutes round-trip if you go at a relaxed pace. If you stop for photos (and you probably will), it might take a bit longer. There's no entrance fee and no crowds—on weekdays, you may only pass a few locals walking their dogs or joggers enjoying the fresh air.

Practical Tips:
Bring a bottle of water and maybe a small snack. There's no shade once you reach the top, so a hat and sunscreen are a good idea, especially in warmer months. I once hiked it in late September, and while the sun wasn't too harsh, the light breeze made it feel just right. Surprisingly, I saw wild boar tracks on the dirt path—apparently, they come out more often at night.

At the summit, there are spots to sit and take in the view. It's a great place for a picnic, a photo shoot, or just a quiet moment to appreciate nature. Some local photographers even come here for sunrise time-lapses.

Additional Info:
There are no facilities at the top, so plan accordingly. You can combine the hike with a visit to nearby **Calamosca Beach**—bring your swimsuit for a post-hike swim. The beach is calm, small, and very local, so it's a great way to round off your outdoor morning.

Villa di Tigellio

Tucked away in the heart of the city, Villa di Tigellio is a quiet archaeological site that gives visitors a unique look at Roman life in Cagliari. Unlike bigger tourist attractions, this site feels personal and uncrowded. It's perfect for those who enjoy history, ancient architecture, or just want a peaceful place to explore.

Address: Via San Saturnino, 21
Price: €5 entry
Activities: Explore Roman ruins, view mosaic floors, learn about ancient life
How to Get There: Take Bus #4 from Largo Carlo Felice and get off near Via San Saturnino. From there, it's just a short 5-minute walk to the entrance.
Best Time to Visit: Late afternoon is best, especially during golden hour when sunlight casts long shadows across the ancient columns.

Why You Should Visit:
Most tourists walk right past this place without realizing it's there. That's part of what makes it so special. The ruins are believed to be the remains of several Roman houses dating back to the 1st century AD. You'll see columns, sections of

stone walls, and beautifully preserved mosaic floors that hint at the lives of the people who once lived here.

When I visited, I was the only person there. It felt like stepping into a forgotten chapter of history. The quiet made it easy to imagine what life might have been like centuries ago—Roman citizens gathering for meals, children playing in the courtyards, and servants moving between rooms.

Guided Experience:
On weekends, local archaeologists or historians sometimes offer guided tours, which are well worth it. One guide told me that the villa's owner was probably a wealthy merchant who loved to entertain. He even had a special courtyard built just for open-air dinners, likely featuring seafood like sea bream and mullet caught nearby. Sardinians take their food seriously—and apparently, so did the Romans.

Practical Tips:
Because the site is not as polished as bigger Roman ruins in Italy, you should wear shoes suitable for uneven ground. The pathways are gravel, and there's not a lot of shade, so a hat and sunglasses help on sunny days.

Photography is allowed, and the lighting in the late afternoon is perfect for catching the details in the mosaics. You can also combine this visit with a walk to nearby **San Saturnino Basilica**, which is just a few blocks away.

Additional Info:
There's a small entrance booth with maps available in English and Italian. The site is not wheelchair-accessible, but it's manageable for most travelers. Toilets and refreshments aren't available here, but several cafes are located a short walk away, making it easy to grab a drink afterward and reflect on what you've just seen.

Calamosca Beach

When you think of beaches in Cagliari, Poetto often comes to mind first. But just a little further along the coast is **Calamosca Beach**, a small, sheltered spot tucked between rugged cliffs. It's less known to tourists, making it ideal if you're looking to relax away from crowds.

Address: Via Calamosca, 09126 Cagliari
Price: Free
Activities: Swimming, snorkeling, beachcombing
How to Get There: Take **Bus #5** from Piazza Matteotti to the **Calamosca** stop. From there, follow signs or simply walk down the short path to the shore.
Best Time to Visit: Weekdays in **June or September** are ideal. You'll avoid the heavy summer crowds and still enjoy warm weather.

What makes Calamosca special is how peaceful it feels. The beach is nestled in a cove, with clear turquoise water gently lapping at the shore. The cliffs around it add to the sense of privacy. On my first visit, I went in late afternoon and found only a handful of locals reading, swimming, or enjoying a quiet break. The water is shallow near the shore, making it good for casual swimming or floating.

If you enjoy **snorkeling**, bring your gear — the rocky areas around the cove are home to small fish and sea urchins. The beach itself is part sand, part pebbles, so wearing water shoes can help. It's also a great place to **beachcomb** — you might find small shells or interesting stones along the tide line.

There are **no lifeguards**, so be mindful if you're swimming, especially with children. The beach does have some shaded spots under rocks or nearby trees, but it's smart to bring an umbrella or hat.

Before heading back, stop at the **gelateria near the bus stop**. I highly recommend the pistachio gelato — it's creamy, rich, and just right after a day in the sun.

Overall, Calamosca is a perfect place for a half-day getaway if you want something more laid-back and scenic than the main beaches. Bring water, a snack, and something to read, and you've got yourself a quiet escape in one of Cagliari's best-kept secrets.

Grotta della Vipera

Tucked in a quiet part of Cagliari, **Grotta della Vipera** is a fascinating yet often-overlooked site. It's an ancient Roman tomb carved into solid rock and surrounded by mystery and local legend. If you enjoy archaeology or unique, lesser-known sites, this is worth your time.

Address: Via XX Settembre (signposted from Parco di Molentargius)
Price: Free
Activities: Exploring an underground Roman tomb
How to Get There: Start from the **Parco di Molentargius** parking lot. From there, it's about a **20-minute walk**. Look for signs pointing to the cave, or ask a local for directions.
Best Time to Visit: Around **midday**, when the sun is high. Light enters the cave and creates a dramatic effect on the stone walls.

The cave's name, "**Grotta della Vipera**," translates to "Cave of the Viper." There are various stories about how it got this name. One local tale says the cave is guarded by a ghostly viper, which gives the place an eerie reputation — especially among children growing up nearby.

The tomb itself dates back to the **1st century AD** and is believed to have been built for a Roman noblewoman named Atilia Pomptilla. She was said to have died from grief after her husband was exiled to Sardinia. The couple's tragic love story is etched into the tomb's walls in Latin script, still visible after nearly 2,000 years.

Inside the cave, the space is tight, and the stone walls are cool to the touch. There is no artificial lighting, so **bring a small flashlight or use your phone light** to see better inside. I visited once during a cloudy afternoon, and the dim light added to the quiet, almost haunting feeling of the space.

The area around the tomb is usually calm. You might see locals jogging or walking their dogs in the nearby park. It's a good stop to pair with a visit to **Molentargius Park**, where you can see flamingos and salt flats — giving your day both natural and historical highlights.

Tip: Wear sneakers or good walking shoes. The **floor inside the cave can be uneven and a bit slippery** from moisture.

Grotta della Vipera is one of those places where history feels very close — no ticket lines, no crowds, just ancient walls and whispers of the past. It's a reminder that Cagliari isn't just beaches and views — it's also full of quiet stories waiting to be found.

Monte Urpinu Park

Monte Urpinu Park is one of the best spots in Cagliari to slow down and take a break from the busier parts of the city. It's a large public park that stretches over one of the city's hills, offering beautiful views and peaceful trails. Whether you're visiting with kids, alone, or with friends, this park gives you a quiet place to relax while also offering a look at how locals spend their free time.

Address: Via XX Settembre, 09129 Cagliari
Price: Free
Activities: Picnics, birdwatching, cityscape photography
How to Get There: Take bus #3 or #8 and get off at the "Monte Urpinu" stop. From there, the park entrance is just a short walk away.
Best Time to Visit: Late afternoon is perfect, especially during the golden hour when the sun starts to set and the light turns warm and soft.

Why You Should Visit:
Monte Urpinu is not just a park; it's a natural balcony overlooking the city. When you reach the top, you'll see panoramic views that stretch across Cagliari's rooftops, the salt flats of Molentargius, and even the sparkling sea in the distance. You'll likely spot flamingos wading through the saltwater ponds below — a unique sight that you don't expect to see in a city park.

The park is filled with pine trees, shady paths, and benches, making it a nice place for a walk or a picnic. There's also a playground area for kids and open lawns where people often walk their dogs or go for light jogs. You'll see locals chatting on benches, teens taking selfies with the city view behind them, and visitors like yourself soaking in the calm.

Personal Tip:
When I visited Monte Urpinu, I brought a sketchpad and ended up staying for

hours. There was something calming about sitting under the trees with the sound of birds in the background. I grabbed a cappuccino from the small café at the top — not fancy, but perfect — and watched the sunset slowly paint the buildings in gold. It's one of those moments where you feel fully present, and that's what travel should be about.

Additional Info:
There's no entry fee, and the park is open all day. It's not crowded, especially on weekdays, and it's easy to find quiet corners to yourself. Bring water and maybe a snack if you're planning to stay a while. The park is safe, well-maintained, and a great place to take a break during your sightseeing day.

Chiesa di Sant'Efisio

Chiesa di Sant'Efisio might not look grand on the outside, but it holds a special place in the hearts of the people of Cagliari. This small church is dedicated to Sardinia's patron saint, Sant'Efisio, and plays an important role in local religious and cultural life. It's simple, peaceful, and rich in tradition — a hidden spot where you can connect with the island's soul.

Address: Via Sant'Efisio, 09124 Cagliari
Price: Free
Activities: Admire Baroque architecture, learn about Sardinia's patron saint
How to Get There: From Largo Carlo Felice, walk about 10 minutes south, following the signs toward the Marina area. It's tucked into a quieter street, so keep an eye out.
Best Time to Visit: May 1st is the most special time — the church becomes the starting point of the annual Sant'Efisio procession, a major local celebration. But if you prefer quiet, go on a weekday morning.

Why You Should Visit:
This church is about stories, faith, and local pride. Inside, the atmosphere is calm and deeply respectful. You'll find candles lit by worshippers, small details in the woodwork, and a statue of Sant'Efisio dressed in traditional garments. The church is small, so you can see everything in about 15–20 minutes, but the experience stays with you much longer.

Sant'Efisio is more than just a religious figure here — he's seen as a protector of the city. In 1652, during a deadly plague, the people prayed to him for help. According to tradition, the city was spared, and ever since, the annual procession honors that moment. Even if you're not religious, it's hard not to feel the emotion and respect surrounding this place.

Personal Tip:
During my visit, I met an elderly man near the church entrance. He noticed I was a visitor and began telling me, in slow but passionate Italian, the story of Sant'Efisio's journey to Nora. He even pointed out a small wooden relic box said to hold sandalwood from the saint's final walk. Moments like that — unexpected, genuine connections — are what make travel special. Don't be afraid to start a conversation or ask a question; the people here are warm and proud of their traditions.

Additional Info:
The church is free to enter and usually open to the public every day, except during private services. It's not wheelchair accessible due to the steps at the entrance. Modest dress is appreciated. If you happen to be in Cagliari during the May Day festival, arrive early — it gets crowded quickly. You'll see traditional dress, music, and even oxen-drawn carts. But on a quiet day, this small church becomes a peaceful space for reflection.

Museo d'Arte Siamese

Tucked inside one of Cagliari's quieter buildings on **Via Roma**, the **Museo d'Arte Siamese** (Museum of Siamese Art) is not a place you'd accidentally stumble across, which makes it even more special. Many locals don't even know it exists, yet it holds one of the most unique collections in Italy—original Thai art and artifacts from the 19th and early 20th centuries. If you're someone who enjoys uncovering unexpected cultural treasures, this small museum is worth a stop.

Address: Via Roma, 115
Price: €6 per adult
Activities: Browse ancient Siamese swords, jewelry, religious statues, musical instruments, and royal gifts

How to Get There: A short 5-minute walk from **Piazza Costituzione**. Look for the entrance near the Citadel of Museums.
Best Time to Visit: Weekdays, around 10–11 AM, to avoid crowds.

The museum is part of the broader collection belonging to **Stefano Cardu**, a Sardinian diplomat and explorer who spent years in Southeast Asia during the late 1800s. He developed a deep admiration for Thai culture and brought back hundreds of rare items. When he passed away, his family donated the collection to the city, and today it quietly sits here, waiting for curious visitors to discover it.

Inside, you'll find finely carved **Buddhist sculptures**, delicate **textiles**, and **decorative daggers** used by Thai nobles. One room contains intricately crafted **ivory and silver boxes**—gifts once exchanged between diplomats or used in royal ceremonies. What makes this museum feel special is how close you can get to each item. There's no sense of distance or glass-heavy display cases. You're walking through someone's passion project, not a sterile gallery.

When I visited, I spent nearly an hour in front of a single silk tapestry, tracing the threads with my eyes and thinking about the artisan who might've worked on it a century ago. The museum is quiet and air-conditioned—perfect for a break from Cagliari's summer heat.

Why You Should Visit:
It's one of the few places in Europe where you can see authentic Thai culture preserved so thoughtfully. If you've never been to Thailand, this collection offers a glimpse. And if you have, it will bring back memories in the best way. Plus, it's something completely different from the Roman ruins and medieval towers scattered around Cagliari.

Additional Info:
There's an **audio guide** available in both **English and Italian**, included with your ticket. The staff are friendly but usually speak limited English, so the guide is helpful. Photography isn't allowed in some areas, so make sure to ask before snapping pictures.

Marina Piccola

Marina Piccola, which means "Little Marina," sits at the southern end of **Poetto Beach**, and it's one of those places that feels far from tourism even though it's just minutes from central Cagliari. Here, locals go about their everyday routines—fishermen mending nets, families walking their dogs, couples watching the sunset with gelato in hand. If you're craving a slice of authentic daily life by the sea, this is the spot.

Address: Lungomare Poetto, Cagliari
Price: Free
Activities: Walk the marina, take photos of boats, talk to local fishermen, and sample fresh seafood
How to Get There: Catch **Bus #5** from **Piazza Matteotti** to the final stop at **Poetto**. From there, walk about 10 minutes south along the coast.
Best Time to Visit: Early evening, especially between **5 PM – 7 PM**, when the light is golden and the fishermen return with the day's catch.

Marina Piccola is not flashy or luxurious—it's modest and full of character. You'll see **colorful fishing boats** rocking gently in the water, older men playing cards in the shade, and food stalls with handwritten menus serving up **fresh grilled fish**, calamari, and sometimes sea urchin when it's in season.

One of my most memorable moments in Cagliari happened right here. I met an older fisherman who was scaling a tuna with a knife that looked almost as old as him. After a quick chat in broken Italian (and a few laughs), he invited me to watch how he grilled the tuna using olive oil, salt, and wild herbs he picked nearby. The flavor was incredible, and I've been using his simple recipe ever since. That kind of hospitality is something you can't schedule—it just happens here.

Why You Should Visit:
This is where the people of Cagliari come to relax. It's not built for tourists, which is exactly why it's worth your time. You'll see what life by the sea really looks like—kids jumping off docks, friends sharing stories, and old boats coming in from a hard day's work.

Additional Info:

- Bring cash if you want to buy fish or snacks; most stalls don't accept cards.
- There are benches all along the walkway, so it's a good place to take a break after a beach day.
- For a quiet morning walk, come before 9 AM when the marina is just waking up.
- The nearby ice cream stand serves a fantastic **pistachio gelato**, and it's popular with locals.

Quartiere Villanova:

Tucked away just below the more touristy Castello district, **Villanova** is one of Cagliari's oldest neighborhoods and feels like an entirely different world. While the Castello might impress with its viewpoints and museums, Villanova charms you with its simplicity—narrow lanes, pastel-colored houses, flower pots hanging from windows, and the quiet rhythm of local life. It's not a place for big attractions, but that's exactly why it's so special.

Address: North of Castello, around Via Università
Price: Free
Activities: Wandering, photography, visiting small local shops and churches

How to Get There

Start your walk from **Largo Carlo Felice**, a central square where many buses stop. Head up toward the Castello and then follow signs or paths leading to the **north side**, where you'll naturally flow into Villanova. The neighborhood is best explored on foot.

Best Time to Visit

Try to go in the **morning**, around 8 or 9 AM. You'll see shutters creaking open, old women chatting from balconies, and the smell of coffee drifting from small bakeries. It's a great time to get a feel for the everyday lives of Cagliari's residents.

What Makes It Special

Villanova is a quiet, local place. The buildings are **low and colorful**, with painted doors and plants everywhere—some staircases are even covered in flowerpots. There are **tiny artisan shops**, especially along streets like **Via San Giovanni**, where locals sell handmade jewelry, woven fabrics, and soaps. These aren't touristy stalls—they're part of the community.

You might also stumble upon a **small church** like **San Giovanni Battista**, which sits quietly among the homes. It's not grand, but locals stop by for prayer, and the cool stone walls provide a break from the Sardinian sun.

Personal Tip

On my last visit, I turned down a small arched alley and ended up in a **hidden courtyard** where two neighbors were having coffee under a vine-covered pergola. They waved, smiled, and one offered me a biscotto. It's that kind of neighborhood—**warm, welcoming, and slow-paced**.

Additional Info

Villanova has something locals call **"porticcioli"**—small archways that connect different parts of the neighborhood. If you're a photographer, these arches create great frames for your shots. Just walk slowly and be respectful; people live here, and the peaceful vibe is what makes it special.

Is Mirrionis Street Art:

If you want to see a different side of Cagliari—something more urban, creative, and full of energy—head to **Is Mirrionis**. This neighborhood may not appear in many tourist brochures, but it's become a hub for **street art** and community expression. Instead of beaches or ruins, here you'll find bold colors, strong messages, and a modern voice for Sardinia's youth.

Address: Via San Gottardo and surrounding streets
Price: Free
Activities: Exploring murals, photography, cultural discovery

How to Get There

Take **Bus #14** from the city center (you can catch it near Piazza Yenne or Via Roma) and ride to the **San Gottardo** stop. From there, just walk. The murals are spread out across the neighborhood, and every few streets you'll discover another wall transformed into art.

Best Time to Visit

Since the murals are all **outdoors**, you can go any time. Midday offers better lighting for photos, but late afternoon brings more locals out onto the streets, adding life to your walk.

What Makes It Special

Is Mirrionis used to be seen as a rougher part of town, but in recent years, it's changed—largely thanks to community-led art projects. Young artists, many from Sardinia, were given walls and the freedom to paint stories, memories, struggles, and hopes. The result is a kind of **open-air art gallery**, and it's raw, honest, and very powerful.

You'll find **murals that celebrate Sardinian culture**, like women in traditional dress or scenes from village life. Others tackle **social topics**—youth identity, environment, or migration. Some are abstract, while others are detailed portraits. One particularly striking mural on **Via San Gottardo** shows a Sardinian jazz musician with a trumpet that seems to pour out birds—it's beautiful and moving.

Personal Experience

While exploring, I followed a narrow street off the main road and found a **small upstairs bar**, nearly hidden. The owner was playing live jazz with two friends. I had a drink, sat near the window, and watched the sun set behind the buildings. It was one of the most unexpected and real moments I've had in Cagliari.

Additional Info

There's no official map posted in the area, but if you visit the **Cagliari tourism website**, you might find downloadable walking routes. Still, part of the charm is wandering without a plan. Just go where your curiosity leads. Wear comfortable shoes, and if you're unsure about direction, ask someone—locals are usually happy to help.

Chapter 4: Outdoor Adventures and Nature

Hiking the Devil's Saddle (Sella del Diavolo) Trail

If you're someone who enjoys a scenic walk with a bit of challenge and a big reward at the top, then the **Devil's Saddle hike** is a must when visiting Cagliari. This iconic ridge sits at the end of Poetto Beach and offers some of the best views in the area. The trail combines coastal beauty, light physical activity, and local legend, all in one memorable route.

- **Address:** Capo Sant'Elia, 09126 Cagliari CA
- **Price:** Free
- **Activities:** Moderate-difficulty coastal hike with panoramic views
- **How to get there:** Take bus 1 or 5 from Cagliari city center to the "Marina Piccola" stop. From there, walk about 10 minutes toward the east. You'll find signs and a dirt path leading up the hill.
- **Best time to visit:** Late spring (May–June) and early autumn (September) are the best months. Temperatures are pleasant, and the trail isn't crowded. Try to start early in the morning or late in the afternoon for cooler weather and great lighting.

Why visit?
The name "Sella del Diavolo" translates to "Devil's Saddle," and it comes from a local legend about a battle between angels and the devil. From the top, you'll understand why it's a favorite among both locals and tourists. You'll see a panoramic view of the **Gulf of Angels**, the long stretch of **Poetto Beach**, the lagoon with flamingos, and even the island of **Serpentara** on a clear day. It's one

of those places where you stop often—not just to catch your breath, but because every corner seems to offer a new photo-worthy view.

Additional info & personal note:
This trail is about 1.5 km each way and takes 45-60 minutes roundtrip, depending on your pace and how often you stop. It starts with a short uphill walk on a gravel path, followed by a few steps carved into the rock. It's not a hard hike, but **you'll want proper walking shoes**. The first part is fully exposed to the sun, so it's smart to bring **a hat, sunscreen, and at least 1 liter of water**.

One morning, I set off just after sunrise. The path was empty, and I could hear only my own steps and the distant waves below. When I reached the first lookout, the sky was painted in soft pink and orange, with the sea perfectly still below. It was one of the most peaceful starts to a day I've ever had.

Cycling Along Poetto's Coastal Path

If you're looking for a relaxing way to explore the coast while staying active, **cycling along the Poetto promenade** is a fantastic choice. The bike path runs parallel to the beach for nearly 8 kilometers, offering open views of the sea, beach bars, and natural scenery. It's a smooth ride that suits all fitness levels, and you can go at your own pace.

- **Address:** Poetto Beach promenade, starting near Via Lungomare Poetto 100
- **Price:** Bike rental costs around €12-€18 for a full day. If you prefer a guided tour, prices start at €30 for a 2-hour ride.
- **Activities:** Leisurely bike ride with stops at beach cafés, scenic points, and natural areas
- **How to get there:** From the city center (Piazza Yenne), take **bus 9** to the "Poetto – Primo Lido" stop. Once you arrive, you'll see several bike rental stands along the promenade.

Best time to visit:
The ideal time for cycling is **early morning or late afternoon**, especially during

the hot summer months. Between July and August, temperatures can reach 30°C or more by midday, so avoid the hottest hours. In the cooler months, anytime between 9 AM and 5 PM is comfortable.

Why visit?
This route is great for soaking in the beach vibe without needing to sit still. You can stop anywhere along the way—maybe grab a cold drink at a kiosk, check out **Molentargius Park** with its flamingos, or just enjoy the fresh breeze from the sea. Since the path is flat and separated from traffic, it's also perfect for families or less experienced riders.

Additional info & personal note:
There are plenty of spots to stop, lock up your bike, and enjoy the surroundings. I like to pause about halfway through the ride at **Il Gabbiano**, a local café right by the water. Last time, I treated myself to a slice of **carasau bread** with **pecorino cheese**—a simple yet satisfying Sardinian snack. I remember the salty air, the distant sound of waves, and the gentle breeze—those small moments that make a trip special.

Don't forget to **bring a reusable water bottle**, **wear sunscreen**, and **carry a map or use your phone GPS**. Although the path is straightforward, some of the side routes into the park or toward small coves can be easy to miss if you're not paying attention.

Birdwatching at Molentargius Natural Park

If you're looking for a peaceful outdoor activity that combines nature, wildlife, and a bit of unexpected beauty in the middle of the city, **Molentargius Natural Park** is the perfect place to go. Located between the city of Cagliari and Poetto Beach, this park is one of Europe's few urban wetlands. It used to be an important site for salt production, but now it's known for its birdlife—especially the striking pink flamingos.

Address: Viale Poetto 126, 09126 Cagliari CA
Price: Free; guided birdwatching tours are available for around €15 per person
Activities: Birdwatching, photography, walking trails, cycling paths

How to get there: Take bus 5 or 6 from the city center to the stop marked "Molentargius." From there, follow the signs to the entrance of the park. It's a short walk, and the area is easy to navigate.

Best time to visit: October to March is the best time if you want to see large flocks of flamingos. April and May are great too because that's when many migratory birds stop by the wetlands.

The park is large, covering over 1,600 hectares, with different zones like salt pans, freshwater pools, and reed beds. These varied environments make it a haven for over 200 bird species. On my visit in February, I joined a small guided walk. The guide handed us binoculars and pointed out different species, including grey herons, moorhens, and of course, the elegant flamingos. What surprised me most was how easy it was to forget you were still in the city—the sounds of traffic were replaced by bird calls and rustling reeds.

One of the highlights is the **pink flamingos**, which are often seen wading through the shallow saltwater ponds. It's a surreal scene, especially with the city skyline in the background. We learned how to tell juvenile flamingos apart from adults—the younger ones have grey feathers that slowly turn pink over time due to the food they eat.

There are plenty of benches and shaded areas where you can take a break, and the park paths are suitable for walking or cycling. However, be sure to wear **sturdy shoes**, especially if it has rained recently—some areas can get muddy. If you're into photography, bring a zoom lens for close-up shots of the birds. And even if you're not an expert birder, the sight of flamingos in flight is something you won't forget.

If you're short on time or traveling with kids, a one-hour visit still gives you a good experience. But if you're a nature lover or someone who enjoys slow travel, you could easily spend half a day exploring different trails and watching the wildlife.

Whether you're visiting for a quick escape from the city or spending a few hours immersed in nature, Molentargius offers a calm and rewarding outdoor experience that doesn't require leaving town.

Kayaking & Stand-Up Paddleboarding around Cagliari Bay

If you're more into active water adventures, then **kayaking or paddleboarding around Cagliari Bay** is a fantastic way to see the coast from a new angle. The calm, clear waters and rocky limestone cliffs make it one of the best spots for beginners and experienced paddlers alike. Plus, it's a fun way to cool off during the warmer months.

Address: Marina Piccola kayak center, Via Cristoforo Colombo 41, 09126 Cagliari CA
Price: Kayak rental from €20/hour; Stand-Up Paddleboard (SUP) rental from €25/hour.
Activities: Kayaking, stand-up paddleboarding, exploring coves, spotting marine life
How to get there: Catch bus 1 from Cagliari's city center to the "Marina Piccola" stop. From there, it's just a short walk to the beach and rental huts.
Best time to visit: May through October is the ideal time, when sea temperatures are warm and conditions are generally calm.

Marina Piccola is the launching point for most rentals. It's a small, well-equipped harbor where you'll find several local businesses offering kayak and paddleboard rentals. You can go out on your own or take a short intro session if you've never done it before. Most renters provide you with safety gear like life vests and dry bags for your belongings.

A popular route is to paddle east along the coast toward **Sella del Diavolo (The Devil's Saddle)**. The cliffs here are rugged and beautiful, and you can often spot small fish through the crystal-clear water beneath your boat. One hidden gem along the route is the **Grotta Verde**, or Green Cave. It's only accessible by kayak or SUP. I visited with a friend last summer around noon, and as we entered the cave, sunlight streamed through the water, lighting it up in bright green hues. It felt like we'd discovered a secret spot straight out of a movie.

Another advantage of paddling in this area is how quiet it is compared to busier parts of the beach. Once you move away from the harbor, all you hear is the splash of your paddle and the occasional call of a gull. It's also not uncommon to see schools of fish or even small jellyfish (don't worry—they're harmless).

Before heading out, make sure to **wear a good sunscreen**, preferably reef-safe, and bring **a waterproof phone case** if you want to take photos. A lightweight long-sleeve shirt and a hat will help protect you from the sun. You don't need to be super fit for this activity, but a bit of arm strength does help, especially if the current picks up.

It's best to go in the morning or late afternoon when the water is calm and the sun isn't too strong. If you're nervous about paddling alone, you can ask about **group excursions or beginner lessons** at the rental station.

Whether you're gliding across the bay solo or with friends, kayaking and paddleboarding offer a unique way to experience Cagliari's coastline—one that most visitors never try. It's peaceful, scenic, and gives you a sense of freedom that few other activities can match.

Snorkeling & Diving near Calamosca

If you're looking for a simple yet exciting water activity in Cagliari, snorkeling and diving near Calamosca is a great place to start. This quiet little bay offers clear water, gentle waves, and easy access, making it perfect for beginners and casual swimmers.

Calamosca Beach is tucked away on the edge of Cagliari and has a peaceful, protected cove. You'll find the water here calm and inviting—ideal conditions for exploring underwater life without needing to go far from the shore. The beach sits at **Via Calamosca, 09126 Cagliari CA**, and is easy to reach by taking **Bus 9** from the city center. Once you get off at the "Calamosca" stop, it's just a **5-minute walk downhill** through a quiet neighborhood to the beach.

The main activities here are **snorkeling and beginner diving lessons**. Snorkeling gear is affordable to rent, usually around **€10 per day**, and there are rental stands or small beach shops nearby that offer masks, fins, and snorkels. For those interested in diving, local dive centers offer **introductory scuba dives for around €60**, which includes basic gear and a short training session.

Under the surface, you'll find **Posidonia oceanica**, also known as Neptune grass. This underwater plant is essential to the Mediterranean ecosystem, and Calamosca is one of the best places in the city to see it. Among the grass beds, you'll likely spot **tiny colorful fish**, sea urchins, and **starfish** clinging to the rocks. The water is shallow and clear, especially from **June to September**, when visibility often reaches up to **15 meters**—a great window for underwater photography.

Why visit? The beach is quieter than Poetto, giving it a more local feel. It's not overly crowded, and the protected bay keeps swimmers safe from strong waves. Whether you're just floating on the surface with a mask or diving a little deeper, the underwater world at Calamosca feels close and accessible.

Personal Note: I tried my first-ever dive at Calamosca. I was nervous, but the instructor was calm and clear. As we moved along a rocky outcrop, I saw a school of **damselfish darting between crevices**, their silver scales catching the light like tiny mirrors. It felt like entering another world—but just minutes from the city. One important tip: **always check the weather forecast** before going. Strong winds or waves can stir up the sand and reduce visibility significantly.

Bring a towel, sun protection, and some cash—there are no ATMs nearby, and some places still prefer cash payments. There's also a small kiosk where you can grab a drink or sandwich after your swim. If you're someone who enjoys peaceful spots and wants to get close to nature without going far, Calamosca is a must.

Exploring Monte Urpinu's Forest Trails

If you're looking for a break from the beach and city noise, **Monte Urpinu** is where you'll find fresh air, quiet paths, and panoramic views. It's the city's most loved green space—ideal for light hikes, nature walks, or just a relaxed afternoon picnic.

Located along **Viale Regina Margherita, 09123 Cagliari**, Monte Urpinu is very easy to get to. You can catch **Bus 4 or 8** and get off at the **"Monte Urpinu" stop**, which drops you directly at the park entrance. From there, winding paths lead you into shaded forest areas and open lookout points.

The park is **free to enter** and is open year-round, but **spring (March to May)** is one of the best times to visit. During these months, **wildflowers bloom** along the trails, and the weather is mild—perfect for walking. Autumn is another great season to explore, especially for photographers who want to capture soft light and fewer visitors.

Monte Urpinu is not a mountain in the typical sense—more of a hill covered in **pine and eucalyptus trees**, with a mix of **gravel paths, stairways, and paved walkways**. The highest points offer **beautiful views** over the city, Molentargius Park, and the Gulf of Angels. If you're someone who enjoys **jogging**, this park has wide open paths where many locals run in the morning. For those more interested in **birdwatching**, you might spot **parakeets, blackbirds, and even hawks** from the upper clearings.

There are also **benches and shaded picnic areas** scattered around the park, so bring some food and enjoy a quiet lunch under the trees. Toward the center of the park, there's a small **duck pond** where families often stop to feed the birds. It's a peaceful place to sit and relax.

Why visit? It's one of the few places in Cagliari where you can feel completely surrounded by nature while still being within the city. Whether you want exercise, fresh air, or a calm place to read a book, Monte Urpinu has a little bit of everything. And best of all—it's free.

Personal Note: On a sunny Sunday afternoon, I stumbled into a small group practicing **tai chi under the pine trees**. It was such a calm and unexpected moment that I ended up joining them for 15 minutes. There were no signs, no schedules—just a group of locals doing their thing in the open air. It reminded me how public spaces like this serve as more than just parks—they're part of the daily life of Cagliari.

Before you go, wear **comfortable shoes**, bring **a water bottle**, and maybe pack a **light jacket** if you're visiting in the evening—it can get breezy at the top. And don't forget your phone or camera; the views from the lookouts are some of the best in the city.

Windsurfing & Sailing on the Gulf of Angels

If you're looking for an active way to enjoy the sea in Cagliari, windsurfing or sailing on the Gulf of Angels is a great choice. The area is known for its steady breeze, calm waves, and wide-open waters—ideal for beginners and experienced water sports lovers alike. Whether you want to try your first windsurf lesson, enjoy a quiet sail at sunset, or take a catamaran out for a spin, the Gulf of Angels provides the perfect setting.

Poetto Windsurf Center, located at **Lungomare Poetto 65**, is one of the most popular spots for rentals and lessons. Windsurf boards are available to rent for about **€25 per hour**, and if you're new to the sport, a **2-hour beginner's lesson** costs around **€50**. For sailing enthusiasts, **half-day lessons** or short catamaran trips are also available for about **€70**. The staff speaks English and Italian and are happy to help you choose the right equipment or guide you through your first time out on the water.

Getting there is simple. From **Cagliari city center**, take **bus 9** to "**Poetto Primo Lido**". From the bus stop, walk along the beach promenade heading south, and you'll find the windsurf center after about 10 minutes. The walk is pleasant, with views of the sea and the beach cafés that line the shore.

The best months for wind-based sports here are between **March and September**, when the **Maestrale wind** blows regularly. This wind is gentle enough for beginners but consistent enough for longer sailing routes and tricks on the board. Mornings tend to be calmer, while afternoons often bring stronger wind conditions—perfect if you're more experienced or want to improve your skills.

During a trip in **May**, I took a sailing lesson just before sunset. It was peaceful as we pushed away from the beach, and by the time we reached open water, the **sky turned soft pink** behind the Castello district. The city looked quiet from the sea, and I remember thinking how different Cagliari feels from that angle—calm, wide, and free.

Practical tip: Wear **quick-dry clothes**, bring a **hat**, and use **UV-protected sunglasses**—the reflection from the water can be very strong. Don't forget sunscreen and water, especially in summer.

This is one of the best ways to enjoy Cagliari's coastline while staying active and seeing the city from a whole new perspective.

Chapter 5: Food, Markets, and Gastronomy

Must-Try Sardinian Dishes in Cagliari

Cagliari's food scene is built around simple ingredients turned into bold, memorable flavors. In this section, we'll introduce five classic Sardinian dishes, each served in a spot beloved by locals. You'll get all the practical details—where to go, what it costs, when to visit, and why it's worth your time—so you can dive straight into the island's culinary heart.

Malloreddus alla Campidanese

At Trattoria Lillicu, you'll find Malloreddus alla Campidanese, Sardinia's signature pasta. These small, ridged gnocchetti are handmade each morning and tossed in a sauce of local pork sausage, ripe tomatoes, and a touch of saffron. A serving costs €12–€15. It's a 10-minute stroll from Piazza Yenne, so head there around 1 pm for peak freshness. The slightly firm texture of the pasta and the spicy sausage make this dish unforgettable. Wash it down with a glass of Vernaccia di Oristano—its light sweetness balances the heat perfectly.

Zuppa Gallurese

If you need comfort on a cool evening, Ristorante Antica Cagliari's Zuppa Gallurese is the answer. For €8–€10, you get layers of stale country bread soaked in rich beef broth and topped with melted pecorino cheese. Take bus #6 to the San Cosimo stop, then walk two minutes to Piazza San Cosimo 18. This dish shines from October to April when the air turns crisp. Remember, it's more bread than soup, so come hungry. The hearty mix of chewy bread and creamy cheese feels like a warm hug from the island itself.

Porceddu (Suckling Pig)

Porceddu is Sardinia's pride: a young pig roasted slowly over myrtle wood until the skin crackles and the meat stays juicy. At Antica Trattoria Sa Schironada (Via

Stagno 14), a half-pig portion costs €18-€22—perfect for sharing. Take tram T1 to Stazione FS, then walk five minutes. Weekends from 7 pm to 10 pm are prime time, but you must book in advance. When you bite into the crispy skin and tender flesh, you'll understand why this dish is a celebration of local flavors and traditions.

Fregola con Arselle

Fregola is Sardinia's answer to couscous: tiny toasted semolina balls with a nutty bite. At Su Cumbidu (Via Sant'Alenixedda 17), it's paired with fresh clams cooked in white wine for €14-€17 a plate. Catch bus #5 to Sant'Alenixedda and prepare for a short uphill walk. The best window is 2 pm to 4 pm, when the seafood arrives straight from the morning catch. A squeeze of lemon and extra parsley brightens the dish. For shellfish lovers, this combines the coast's briny taste with a satisfying, chewy base.

Seadas

End your meal on a sweet note with a Seada from Pasticceria Piuma at Via Roma 145. For €4-€5, you get a crisp, deep-fried pastry stuffed with pecorino cheese and drizzled in honey. It's just a five-minute walk from Largo Carlo Felice. Stop by between 3 pm and 5 pm for an afternoon treat, ideally paired with a strong espresso. If you can, try the version made with wildflower honey—it adds a fragrant twist that lifts the rich cheese filling into something truly special.

Where to Eat Like a Local:

When you're in Cagliari, nothing beats slipping into a cozy trattoria where recipes pass down through generations. These spots aren't flashy—they're about home cooking, friendly faces, and feeling part of the family. Here's five of the best places to eat like a local, each with its own story and special dishes.

Trattoria L'Antiporto

Nestled on a quiet side street, L'Antiporto serves a fixed menu that changes daily. You'll sit in a simple room filled with family photos and the hum of nearby conversation.

From €15–€20 per person, you get two courses plus a glass of house wine. The first course might be malloreddus in sausage sauce, followed by slow-braised beef with roasted potatoes. To reach it, catch bus #3 to the Via Manno stop—then it's just across the road. Aim for a weekday lunch, when locals fill the tables but the pace stays relaxed. They close at 2:30 pm, so don't wander in after 2 pm or you'll miss out.

Da Gigi

Stepping through Da Gigi's door feels like visiting a Sardinian uncle's home. Owner Gigi greets regulars by name, pours his own red wine, and shares stories as he plate-ups fresh pasta or grills tender cuts of meat.

A meal here costs about €12–€18 per person. Think homemade tagliatelle with seafood or a platter of grilled lamb chops. You'll find it at Via Sulis 27, a ten-minute walk from Piazza Costituzione. Dinner on a weekday evening is ideal—weekends fill up fast, and there's no reservation system. Remember: it's cash only.

Trattoria Castello

Perched just below the castle walls, this trattoria uses a cast-iron grill to sear steaks and seasonal veggies. The room is rustic, with wooden tables and views of the harbor at sunset.

Expect to spend €18–€22 per person on a three-course meal. To get there, take the funicular from the Marina up toward Castello, then follow winding lanes to Salita di Santa Caterina 29. A sunset dinner (around 7 pm) shows you the golden light over the sea. There's no phone to call—arrive by 7 pm to claim a seat before they sell out.

Sa Domu Sarda

Sa Domu Sarda is all about grazing. Long tables are stacked with platters of pecorino, prosciutto, marinated olives, and crusty bread. It's a relaxed spot to sip a glass of Vermentino and chat with neighbors.

With prices from €14–€19 per person, you'll tuck into an antipasto feast. Take bus #1 to Sassari, then walk three minutes down Via Sassari 50. Early evening (6 pm–8 pm) is best—this is aperitivo time in Sardinia. Don't leave without trying their caponata di verdure, a sweet and tangy eggplant stew that pairs perfectly with cheese.

Trattoria Is Caognitive

Simple and hearty, Is Caognitive feels like your grandmother's kitchen. The menu lists one or two soups—maybe a creamy zucchini soup—and a fresh pasta special of the day.

Meals run €10–€15 each. From Largo Carlo Felice, walk seven minutes to Via San Giovanni 39. Lunch hours (12 pm–2 pm) ensure you taste the pasta at its peak, when it's just been pulled and cooked. Portions here are big—come hungry, but save room for a sweet finale.

Top Seafood Spots in the Marina District

Cagliari's Marina District sits right on the old port, a short walk from sandy beaches and bustling markets. Here, you'll find some of the city's best seafood—fresh catches turned into simple, elegant dishes. Whether you're in the mood for a multi-course tasting or a quick plate of fried fish, these five spots deliver the true taste of Sardinia's waters.

1. Ristorante Dal Corsaro

Just steps from the harbor, Dal Corsaro offers a refined take on local seafood. Their tasting menu (around €25–€35 per person) changes daily based on what's fresh. Expect dishes like razor-thin swordfish carpaccio, sea urchin spaghetti, and a light brodetto fish stew. It's a five-minute walk from the port—follow the quay toward Via dei Genovesi. Aim for an 8 pm dinner reservation to dine by candlelight and watch boats bobbing in the harbor. The elegant setting and creative presentations make it worth booking weeks in advance. Locals praise the chef's modern twists, so come ready to try something new.

2. La Vecchia Bottega del Mare

La Vecchia Bottega is a counter-style fish shop turned grill house. Prices hover between €18 and €25 per person, depending on the catch. They keep it simple: the fish of the day is grilled over oak coals, seasoned with a drizzle of local olive oil and a squeeze of lemon. To get there, take Tram T1 to Baylle and walk two minutes down Via Baylle. Lunchtime (1 pm–3 pm) is best—fishermen roll in with fresh boxes of clams, prawns, and whole fish. Pull up a stool at the counter, chat with the chef, and ask what's best that day. The open kitchen feels lively and authentic.

3. Sa Piola

Hidden on Via Don Bosco, Sa Piola is famous for its seafood risotto and octopus carpaccio. A meal here runs about €20–€28 per person. Catch Bus #4 to Don Bosco and walk a minute to find this cozy spot. Arrive early for dinner (7 pm–8 pm) to beat the crowd. The risotto is perfectly al dente, studded with mussels and saffron, while the carpaccio comes draped over a bed of arugula. Their sommelier will suggest Sardinian white wines that cut through the richness. It's a favorite among residents who know their rice.

4. Il Gatto Nero

Tucked down a side street off Via Roma, Il Gatto Nero specializes in fritto misto (mixed fried seafood) and clams steamed in white wine. Budget €16–€22 per person. From Largo Carlo Felice, it's an eight-minute walk past hidden courtyards. Late lunch (2 pm–4 pm) is ideal if you prefer a quieter meal. Their fry is extremely light—shrimp, anchovies, and small squid come out crisp without feeling greasy. The garlic-white wine clams arrive in a shallow bowl that's perfect for mopping up with crusty bread. As a finale, homemade limoncello is served tableside.

5. Ristorante Il Maestrale

Perched near the top of the Castello quarter, Il Maestrale gives you seafood with a view. Expect to spend €22–€30 per person on dishes like grilled swordfish steaks and linguine tossed with baby octopus. Take the funicular up to Castello, then walk five minutes down cobblestone lanes to Via Santa Maria del Toro. Sunset dinners are magic here—terrace seating (when the weather allows) looks out over the city and port. The ingredients come straight from local boats, so every bite tastes of the sea. Just check ahead if the terrace is open before you go.

San Benedetto Market:

San Benedetto Market is one of Europe's largest covered food markets. It's a lively place where locals shop every day. Bright stalls line the aisles, and you'll hear vendors calling out their freshest goods. Whether you're after fruit, seafood, cheese, cured meats, or pantry staples like olive oil and honey, this market has it all. Here's how to make the most of your visit.

1. Fresh Fruit & Veg Stall – Frutta Flora

Start your market trip with color and flavor at Frutta Flora. This stall bursts with produce you won't find at a supermarket. Think prickly fichi d'India (prickly pears) or small blood oranges. Each item costs around €1–€3, so it's easy to sample a few. Vendors often offer tastes—just ask politely. To get here, hop on bus #8 and step off right outside. Aim for 7–9 am when produce is at its peak. Bring small coins or exact change; it speeds up transactions. You'll leave with a bag full of vibrant fruit and a better sense of Sardinian agriculture.

2. Seafood Counter – Pescheria Mari Pintau

Next, head to Hall C, Stall 12, where fresh fish and shellfish arrive daily. Prices run €10–€20 per kilo, depending on the catch. Watch vendors clean and prepare clams, prawns, or octopus right in front of you. They're happy to share cooking tips—ask how to grill or steam your selection. The market sits about a 12-minute walk from the Marina, but you can also follow the signs once inside. Visit between 9–11 am, right after the fishing boats dock. If you plan to take seafood home, they'll pack it on ice. It's an ideal stop for anyone who wants truly fresh ingredients.

3. Cheese Seller – Casearia Sarda

In Hall B at Stall 5, you'll find an array of sheep-milk cheeses. Prices range from €8 to €15 per kilo. Here you can sample smoked pecorino (affumicato), marinated rounds, or young, fresh wheels. The vendor often explains how each cheese is made, sharing the story of local flocks and shepherding traditions. To reach this stall, take the Tram T2 to the Mercato stop and walk inside to Hall B. Visit before noon to see the full selection; many varieties sell out early. Ask for pairing suggestions—local honey or a slice of crusty bread make perfect partners.

4. Charcuterie – Salumi Mamoiada

Just down the aisle in Hall D at Stall 3 is an excellent spot for cured meats. You'll pay €10–€18 per kilo for cuts like spianata (flat salami) or spicy salsiccia sarda. Bus #9 drops you at the market entrance; from there, Hall D is clearly marked. The best time is around lunchtime, 12–2 pm, when you can assemble a quick meat-and-cheese snack on the go. The smoky, savory flavors here define Sardinian charcuterie. Vendors will slice and wrap portions so you can carry them home or enjoy immediately.

5. Olive Oil & Honey – Delizie Mediterranee

Finally, explore pantry essentials at Hall A, Stall 8. Single-estate olive oils and wildflower honeys range €6–€12 per bottle or jar. Bus #7 stops just across the street—perfect for hauling jars back to your accommodation. Visit between 8–10 am when the vendor is most chatty and eager to discuss harvest methods. You'll taste oils pressed from nearby groves and honeys harvested by local beekeepers. These small-batch products make thoughtful gifts; ask for gift packaging if you plan to take them home.

Wine Bars and Regional Varietals

Wine culture in Cagliari goes beyond big-name bottles—you'll find small bars pouring local gems you might never see elsewhere. Below are five favorite spots where you can taste Sardinia's lesser-known reds and whites, learn about local grapes, and pair your glass with small bites. Each place brings its own vibe and expertise, so whether you're a wine novice or a seasoned sipper, you'll walk away with new favorites.

1. Enoteca Cagliaritana

Just off the main drag, this cozy bar is a great entry point to Sardinian wines.

Address: Via Barcellona 9
Price: €5–€10/glass; €20–€30/bottle
Activities: Try a flight of three Sardinian reds or whites—ask the staff to mix reds if you prefer full-bodied wines, or whites if you like something crisp.

How to Get There: Take bus #12 to Via Barcellona, then walk one block.
Best Time: Arrive between 6 pm and 8 pm for happy-hour deals—most flights are discounted by 10–15%.
Why Visit: The staff know their stuff and will guide you toward unusual grapes like Bovale and Pascale.
Additional Info: Small cheese and meat plates (€6–€8) make this a perfect spot to graze while you taste.

2. Cantina di San Biagio

Tucked into Piazza Yenne, this cellar-style bar feels historic and unhurried.

Address: Piazza Yenne 13
Price: €6–€12/glass; €25–€40/bottle
Activities: Sign up for a guided tasting of Carignano del Sulcis DOC—typically a three-wine lineup with notes on each vintage.
How to Get There: A 3-minute walk from Largo Carlo Felice.
Best Time: Weekend afternoons from 3 pm to 5 pm, when the pace is relaxed and you can linger.
Why Visit: They focus on grapes grown just outside Cagliari, and the guides share stories of each vineyard's history.
Additional Info: Ask for the underground cellar tour—it's a cool 15-minute walk through stone-vaulted rooms where barrels rest.

3. Barley Wine Bar

Modern décor meets local flavor at this stylish spot on Via Roma.

Address: Via Roma 105
Price: €7–€14/glass; boutique bottles from €30
Activities: Attend a weekly wine-pairing dinner—seasonal menus match three wines to small plates.
How to Get There: Tram T1 to Via Roma, then two minutes on foot.
Best Time: Thursday evenings are pairing night—reserve ahead to get in.
Why Visit: The tapas are locally sourced—think swordfish bites and mini seadas—that echo the wines you try.
Additional Info: Reservations for pairing dinners fill up fast; call at least two days in advance.

4. Le Cantine Is Maglias

A family home-turned-wine bar where everyone feels welcome.

Address: Via Santa Croce 57
Price: €5–€9/glass; €22–€35/bottle
Activities: Book a 90-minute guided tasting—five Sardinian wines served with light snacks.
How to Get There: Bus #10 to Santa Croce, then a short walk.
Best Time: Late afternoon (5 pm–7 pm) is ideal—you'll finish just in time for dinner.
Why Visit: The owners share firsthand tales of vineyard life, making each pour feel personal.
Additional Info: The tasting fee (€20) includes small bites of pecorino, salami, and bread.

5. Vineria L'Ulivo

Casual meets creative at this relaxed bar near Piazza Yenne.

Address: Via Sassari 21
Price: €4–€8/glass; €18–€28/bottle
Activities: Create your own tasting flight—pick any three wines—and build a cheese board from their counter.
How to Get There: An eight-minute walk from Piazza Yenne.
Best Time: Happy hour (6 pm–8 pm) offers combo deals: €12 for three glasses plus a small board.
Why Visit: With live acoustic music some nights, it feels like you're hanging out in a friend's living room.
Additional Info: No reservations needed—just drop in and choose your wines.

Best Gelaterias in the City

Whether you're craving a classic scoop or something adventurous, each of these gelaterias has its own draw.

Gelateria Artigianale Old Oak

Nestled on a quiet side street, Old Oak keeps things simple and authentic.
Per-scoop Price: €2.50–€4
Highlights: Pistachio di Bronte and Vernaccia sorbet showcase local nuts and wine grapes. They source milk from nearby farms and skip stabilizers, giving their gelato a natural, silky mouthfeel.
Getting There: Take bus #11 to the Santa Croce stop—Old Oak is right across the street.
Best Time to Visit: Late afternoon (4 pm–6 pm), when the gelato is at peak creaminess and the crowds thin out.
Why Go: You get pure, unadulterated flavors made in small batches.
Tip: Ask about the seasonal sorbet—the rotating options often feature fruits picked that morning.

Gelateria Fiore di Latte

Just off Largo Carlo Felice, Fiore di Latte is known for its smooth texture and Sardinian twists.
Per-scoop Price: €2–€3.50
Highlights: Don't miss the Seada-inspired honey gelato or the rich dark chocolate.
Getting There: A seven-minute walk from Largo Carlo Felice through a leafy neighborhood.
Best Time to Visit: Evening (7 pm–9 pm), when locals stroll home after dinner with cones in hand.
Why Go: Their secret is extra-resting time in the freezer, giving each scoop a tender, melt-in-your-mouth quality.
Tip: Order a "coppetta mista" to sample two contrasting flavors together.

Gelato d'amare

A tram ride away, this spot focuses on freshness and variety.
Per-scoop Price: €3–€5
Highlights: Limoncello sorbet and fig-and-almond are standouts, reflecting Sardinia's citrus groves and olive orchards.
Getting There: Tram T1 to Baylle, then a two-minute walk through the market

stalls.
Best Time to Visit: Mid-morning (11 am–1 pm) for short lines and just-made batches.
Why Go: They churn gelato in small runs every few hours to guarantee freshness.
Tip: Vegan and dairy-free options are clearly labeled—ideal if you have dietary needs.

Dolce Sardegna

Located beside San Benedetto Market, this gelateria feels like a market stall for ice cream.
Per-scoop Price: €2–€4
Highlights: Ricotta-and-honey and saffron flavors use ingredients pulled straight from market stalls.
Getting There: A three-minute stroll from the market entrance—follow the gelato aroma!
Best Time to Visit: Around 1 pm when vendors start packing up, making it a perfect post-shopping reward.
Why Go: You'll taste the market's freshest honey swirled right into your cone.
Tip: Ask for a mini cone sampler so you can try two flavors before committing.

Il Gelataio di Via Roma

On a bustling stretch of Via Roma, this gelateria mixes classic tastes with creative combos.
Per-scoop Price: €2.50–€4
Highlights: Sea salt caramel and pear-and-walnut pair unexpected sweet and savory notes.
Getting There: Tram T2 to the Via Roma stop—Il Gelataio is a few steps away.
Best Time to Visit: Afternoon (3 pm–5 pm), when they've just restocked every flavor.
Why Go: Their adventurous twists push the limits of what gelato can be.
Tip: Top your scoop with chopped pistachio for extra crunch and color.

Street Food:

Cagliari's street food scene is a lively mix of quick bites and local favorites. Whether you're rushing between sights or lingering by the sea, these snacks hit the spot. Here's a closer look at five must-try stalls, with tips on when to go, how to get there, and what makes each one special.

1. Panini Porchetta – Street Vendor near Bastione

Just below the Bastione di Saint Remy, this porchetta stall offers the perfect grab-and-go lunch. You'll find it on **Viale Regina Margherita**, right by the bastion walls. For **€5–€6**, the vendor slices warm, herby porchetta and piles it into a crusty roll, sprinkling on fresh rosemary. To reach it, catch **bus #7** to the "Bastione" stop and walk a minute toward the landmark. Aim for **1 pm–3 pm**—the midday rush eases, and the pork stays piping hot. Don't miss the green salsa—its tang cuts through the meat's richness.

2. Arrosticini Stall – Near Poetto Bus Stop

After a day on Poetto Beach, follow the smoke to **Largo Giunco 4**, outside the Poetto bus stop. Here, skewers of **arrosticini**—simple, salt-seasoned lamb—cost just **€1 each** (order at least five). Catch **bus #1** from downtown and hop off at "Poetto." Evenings between **6 pm and 9 pm** are best, when locals queue after the sun dips. Each skewer is charred at the edges yet juicy inside, making it an ideal beach-to-street snack. Note: They sell out quickly and take cash only.

3. Arancini Siciliani – Market Entrance Cart

At the main gates of San Benedetto Market, a cart fries **arancini** fresh each morning. These golden rice balls, filled with ragù or spinach-ricotta, run **€2.50** apiece. To find it, take **bus #8** to the market entrance and look (and smell) for the sizzling oil. Visit between **9 am and 11 am** for the crispiest shells. The ragù version is hearty and rich; spinach-ricotta offers a lighter, tangy bite. It's the perfect pick-me-up between produce stalls and fish counters.

4. Pani Frattau Wrap – Food Truck on Via Roma

On **Via Roma 102**, near Largo Carlo Felice, a bright red food truck serves **pani frattau**—the street version of Sardinian lasagna. Layers of thin, crispy pane carasau are spread with tomato sauce, topped with a fried egg and pecorino flakes. Each wrap costs **€6**. Hop off **tram T1** at "Via Roma" and you're steps away. Visit for **lunch between 12 pm and 2 pm** to see them layering fresh wraps all afternoon. Ask for extra cheese if you love a salty kick.

5. Culurgiones – Outdoor Market Stall

On weekend mornings, a stall pops up in **Piazza Yenne**, selling **culurgiones**—dumplings pinched into little plaits and filled with potato-mint paste and pecorino. A plate of six costs **€8–€10**. It's just a **2-minute walk** from Largo Carlo Felice. Look for it around **9 am–12 pm**, when the market buzz is at its peak. These soft parcels taste like Sardinia's inland hills in every bite. Bring a small container if you want to take extra sauce along for dipping.

Chapter 6: Art, Music, and Cultural Life

Cagliari's Contemporary Art Spaces

Contemporary art in Cagliari is alive and growing, with galleries and project spaces that champion local and international creators. These venues aren't just walls with paintings—they're cultural hubs where you can meet artists, join workshops, and discover Sardinia's vibrant art scene. Below are four standout spots to explore.

Quartiere Ghetto Arte Contemporanea

Just off busy Via San Francesco, this stripped-back warehouse turned gallery is a meeting point for emerging Sardinian artists. You'll find rotating exhibitions of painting, photography, and mixed media, alongside informal artist talks that often pop up in the late afternoon. Drop in for free, or sign up for a weekend workshop (usually €10–€20) where you can try your hand at printmaking or collage. To get here, hop on bus #3 or #14 to the "San Francesco" stop, then walk two minutes down a side street. Aim for around 16:00–18:00, when the light is soft and artists linger over an espresso. Why go? It's grassroots, open, and you'll leave with fresh insights straight from the people making art in Cagliari. Before you visit, check their Instagram for surprise performances or pop-up events.

Galleria Comunale d'Arte

Housed in a modern, white-walled building near the docks, Galleria Comunale d'Arte offers a neat look at Sardinia's modern art scene. Entry is €5 for adults (free under 18), and guided tours run for €3 if you want context on the pieces. School programs bring in groups during the week, so mornings between 10:00 and 12:00 are usually quieter. Take tram T2 to the "Galleria d'Arte" stop and you're seconds away. Inside, a sleek café serves coffee and light bites, making it easy to linger. On the first Sunday of every month, admission is free—great if you're pinching pennies. The gallery's mix of paintings, sculptures, and installations offers an accessible overview of local and Italian mid-century trends.

Exma – Exhibiting and Moving Arts

Exma sits in an old convent on Via San Lucifero, just outside the front door of the bus #1 and #4 stop. For a small fee (€4 standard, €2 reduced), you can wander through video art rooms, catch a multimedia installation, or even stay for a dance performance in the courtyard. Evening events often kick off at 19:00, when the space transforms into an immersive show under soft lighting. Their on-site café ups the fun with themed cocktails inspired by the current exhibit—think neon drinks to match digital projections. Exma's edge lies in its blend of visual and live art. It's where technology meets tradition, and you'll walk away with an experience rather than just a memory.

MAN – Museo d'Arte Provincia di Nuoro (Cagliari Branch)

Though based in Nuoro, MAN's Cagliari branch on Piazza Arsenale brings Sardinia's wider art scene to the capital. From '50s-era modernism to recent works, the museum's provincial collection spans painting, sculpture, and photography. Entry is €6 (students and seniors pay €3), and free lockers keep your backpack safe while you explore. To reach MAN, take bus #8 to "Arsenale" or hop on the ferry-bus from Poetto Beach for a scenic ride. Visit on a midweek morning to avoid school groups. The exhibits change regularly, so you'll often find fresh voices alongside the classics. Visiting MAN gives you a deeper look at how Sardinian artists have engaged with modern art movements over the last seventy years.

Teatro Lirico di Cagliari

Cagliari's Teatro Lirico is more than a building—it's the city's main stage for opera, classical concerts, and jazz events. Its elegant Art Nouveau façade and excellent acoustics draw both locals and visitors. Even if you've never been to an opera, the lively atmosphere and high-quality productions make a night here something special.

1. La Traviata (Verdi)

Verdi's *La Traviata* is one of the world's most beloved operas. When staged at Teatro Lirico, it feels both grand and personal, with each note carried clearly through the hall.

Attending *La Traviata* here starts in the foyer, where a small queue of well-dressed guests checks coats at the cloakroom. Seats range from €15 in the balcony to €80 in the stalls. Look for surtitles projected above the stage in both Italian and English—these help you follow the story. The opera begins at 20:30, so arrive by 19:45 to pick up tickets and grab a program (€2). The best time is opening night, when the cast and orchestra are at their most energized. Take Tram T1 to the "Teatro Lirico" stop and walk two minutes. Smart casual attire is standard; a scarf or blazer will fit in nicely.

2. Cagliari Jazz Festival

Every July, Teatro Lirico transforms into a hub for international jazz. This festival draws big names and local talent, with daytime workshops and late-night jam sessions.

Day passes cost €20, or you can buy a full-festival wristband for €60. Main shows take place on the indoor stage, while good-weather nights spill into the glass-walled foyer with free outdoor seating. Workshops—covering topics from improvisation to sax techniques—are held in adjacent rooms and usually cost €10 each. To get there, catch one of several city buses to the theatre, or hop on the free shuttle from Piazza Yenne. July is ideal: the warm evenings and sea breeze add to the vibe. Don't miss the midnight jam sessions in the foyer, where you can chat with musicians over a craft beer (€5).

3. Symphony Season

From September through November, Teatro Lirico hosts Cagliari's Philharmonic Orchestra. These concerts range from intimate chamber pieces to full symphonic works.

Ticket prices run €10 for upper gallery seats up to €50 for prime orchestra seats. Most performances start at 19:00; pre-concert talks begin at 18:00 in the small lecture hall next door (free with concert ticket). The autumn schedule often includes film-score nights and guest conductors from across Europe. Tram T1 or bus #9 will drop you at "Teatro Lirico." Aim for midweek concerts when the house is quieter—perfect for music lovers who prefer a more reflective experience. The warm glow of the hall's lighting and the crisp fall air make for a cozy evening.

4. Sardinian Song Recitals

For a taste of true Sardinian culture, catch a *cantu a tenore* recital in the intimate Sala Gialla. These vocal performances date back centuries and offer a unique window into local traditions.

Recital tickets are €12–€30, depending on seating. The Sala Gialla seats about 150, so buy your ticket in advance online or at the box office. Shows often start at 21:00 and run about 60 minutes. Bus #14 to "Viale Trieste" is the quickest route. May is the best month—around the Festa di Sant'Efisio, when interest in Sardinian music peaks. Sometimes these recitals include a local wine tasting (€8 extra), pairing cannonau or vermentino with traditional songs. The result is an authentic, memorable evening that blends music and local flavor.

Sardinian Folk Festivals and Traditions

Sardinia holds tightly to its traditions. In Cagliari, you can join lively processions, colorful parades, and music nights that connect you to island life. These events happen at set times each year and draw locals and visitors alike. Below are four key celebrations—each with what to expect and how to make the most of it.

1. Festa di Sant'Efisio

This is Sardinia's most important cultural event. Every May, residents honor Saint Efisio with a 60-day pilgrimage from Cagliari to the church at Nora.

That first weekend in May, you'll see hundreds of people in traditional dress parading along Poetto Beach. The route starts at **Chiesa di Sant'Efisio** and winds through the city. Watching is free. You can hop on **Bus #9** to the "Poetto" stop, then walk a short distance to the church. The best time is **May 1–4**, with the main procession on May 1. Locals carry small gifts—olive branches or candles—to leave at the altar. Join in if you like; handing over a candle is a way to take part in this living tradition.

2. Cagliari Carnival

Carnival in Cagliari brings Europe's grand masked balls down to island level. Throughout February, you'll find parades, costume contests, and workshops for kids.

The main action centers on **Piazza Yenne** and the **Castello** quarter. Street parades are free, but for a more formal masked ball you'll pay **€10-€20**. Take **Bus #4** or **#5** to "Piazza Yenne." The lead-up to Shrove Tuesday is the peak, with the streets packed in the evening. Children under 12 can enter costume contests and win small prizes. For extra fun, drop into one of the free prep workshops in local community centers—great for making your own mask before the big day.

3. Autunno in Barbagia – Cagliari Edition

In October and November, Sardinian villages open their doors for a harvest-time festival. You'll taste chestnut fritters, watch folk dances, and browse artisan stalls.

Events rotate among villages in the Cagliari province, so you'll need a car or book a day-trip bus tour from the city. Entry is free; craft workshops run **€5-€15**. Arrive mid-morning to follow the cooking demos, then stay through the afternoon dances and storytelling around open fires. Wear comfortable shoes—sites can be spread out on uneven streets. This is your chance to meet local families, sample homemade cheeses, and hear stories passed down for generations.

4. Launeddas Music Evenings

Launeddas—the traditional three-pipe reed instrument—fills summer evenings with haunting tunes. Concerts take place in **Piazza San Domenico** during June and July.

Shows are free or ask for a small **€5** donation. To reach Castello, take **Bus #6**, then walk five minutes uphill. Performances start just after sunset, usually around 20:30. The sea breeze can be cool as night falls, so bring a light jacket. Listening to launeddas here isn't just a concert—it's a window into Sardinia's pastoral past, where shepherds would play these pipes to call in their flocks at dusk.

Local Craftsmanship:

Sardinians take pride in handmade goods—every piece tells a story. In Cagliari, small workshops and boutiques keep centuries-old skills alive, mixing traditional methods with fresh designs. Visiting these studios isn't just shopping—it's a glimpse into the island's soul, where you can watch raw materials transform under skilled hands. Below are four top spots to explore—and maybe even try your hand at crafting something of your own.

1. Ceramica Papisca

Step inside a bright studio filled with spinning wheels and painted tiles. Here, the master potter shows you how local clay becomes delicate dishes bearing Cagliari's signature blue-and-white patterns.

- **Address:** Via Maddalena, 13
- **Price:** Souvenirs €15–€60; workshop €25 pp (2 hours)
- **Activities:** Guided demo of wheel throwing, hands-on shaping and decorating
- **How to get there:** Bus #3 to "Maddalena" stop, 2-minute walk
- **Best time to visit:** Weekday mid-mornings, when the potter is free to chat
- **Why visit:** You'll learn the island's classic motifs and take home your own mini vase
- **Additional info:** Reserve workshop spots online at least 48 hours ahead

2. Lanaitessile Textile Studio

Imagine a quiet room at noon, sunlight on wooden looms as skilled weavers thread wool into scarves. At Lanaitessile, you'll see how raw fleece—once scratchy and dull—becomes soft, colorful fabric ready for the runway or your own wardrobe.

- **Address:** Via XX Settembre, 53
- **Price:** Woven scarves €40; weaving workshop €30 (3 hours)

- **Activities:** Live demos of warp and weft techniques, chance to try the loom
- **How to get there:** Bus #14 to "XX Settembre," then a short walk
- **Best time to visit:** Afternoon, when artisans are deep in their work
- **Why visit:** Watch plant-dyed threads take shape and hear stories of old weaving traditions
- **Additional info:** Shop also sells small-batch linens made with local herbs and flowers

3. Coral Art Gallery

Cagliari's red coral is world-famous. At this gallery, you'll see artisans carve bright branches into necklaces and brooches right before your eyes. The shimmer of fresh polish makes each piece feel alive.

- **Address:** Via Sardegna, 28
- **Price:** Jewelry from €50; showroom visits free
- **Activities:** Live carving and polishing demonstrations, guided showroom tour
- **How to get there:** Bus #4 or #7 to "Via Sardegna," then a two-minute walk
- **Best time to visit:** Late morning, just after new pieces are finished
- **Why visit:** Learn why Sardinian coral ranks among the world's finest gems
- **Additional info:** Ask for a behind-the-scenes peek into the carving workshop

4. Su Filu e Su Ferru Blacksmith

Feel the heat and hear the spark as hammers strike glowing metal. At this ironworks studio, traditional tools meet modern designs, turning raw iron into sleek hooks, candles holders, and more.

- **Address:** Piazza Matteotti, 5

- **Price:** Small iron pieces €20–€45; forging demo €10 donation
- **Activities:** Live forging demo, guided chance to shape a simple keepsake
- **How to get there:** Bus #3 to "Matteotti" then a one-minute walk
- **Best time to visit:** Early afternoon, when the forge fire is hottest
- **Why visit:** Watch centuries-old blacksmithing come alive—and leave with a tiny hand-made souvenir
- **Additional info:** Wear closed-toe shoes if you plan to join the demo

The Role of Sardinian Language in Culture

Sardinian isn't just a dialect—it's a living language with roots in ancient Latin. In Cagliari, you'll hear it in poetry readings, see it on street signs, and catch it in everyday chat. It's a proud emblem of Sardinian identity, linking modern life to centuries of history. Below are four ways you can experience Sardinian in action and deepen your connection to the island's culture.

1. Sardinian Poetry Open-Mic

Every Wednesday at **Libreria Cyrano**, local poets gather to share verses in both Sardinian and Italian. The open-mic night starts at **19:30**, and entry is free (you can leave a small **€3 donation** if you like). The intimate bookshop setting invites you to listen closely to the emotion and music of the **Campidanese** dialect. To get there, take **bus #6** to the "Sulis" stop—just a short walk away. Even if you're not a poet, you can soak up the words and, if you feel bold, offer up a few lines of your own.

2. Language Workshops at CUEC

If you want to pick up a few Sardinian phrases, the **CUEC** language center offers a friendly way in. Located at **Via Sassari, 179**, they run **five-week courses** for **€50**, or you can drop in for a single session at **€12**. Classes cover basic vocabulary, pronunciation, and simple conversations. You'll meet in small groups from **September through June**, which means plenty of chances to practice with classmates. Take **bus #2** or **#12** to the "Sassari" stop, then follow signs to the bright yellow CUEC building. By the end, you'll have enough Sardinian to greet shopkeepers, ask for directions, and show respect for local traditions.

3. Sardinian Street Signs Walk

For a free, hands-on tour, head to **Piazza Yenne** on Saturday mornings at **10:00**. A guide leads you through the **Castello** quarter, pointing out bilingual street names and explaining their meanings. The walk lasts about **90 minutes** and is perfect in spring, when flowers bloom around the old palaces. To join, simply hop off **bus #5** at the Piazza Yenne kiosk. You'll learn how Sardinian words like "*Via Logu de Casti*" still mark the city's medieval roots. Wear comfortable shoes, and bring a camera—every corner tells a story.

4. Local Radio "Radio Barbagia" Segments

For a slice of daily life in Sardinian, tune in to **Radio Barbagia** at **98.0 FM** or stream online. Their morning shows run from **08:00 to 10:00**, mixing news bulletins, folk music, and live call-in segments—all in Sardinian. You'll hear farmers calling in, traditional songs, and hosts reading listeners' messages in dialect. There's no cost to listen—just grab your phone or radio and enjoy. This is a great way to tune your ear to local pronunciation and discover how the language lives on across generations.

Live Music Venues and Jazz Bars

When the sun goes down, Cagliari comes alive with music. From smooth jazz to indie rock and late-night DJ sets, these spots offer a taste of the city's vibrant nightlife. Here's a closer look at four must-visit venues.

1. Blue Note Cagliari

If you love jazz, Blue Note Cagliari feels like a small New York club tucked into Sardinia. The low ceiling and cozy tables make every note feel personal.

Blue Note is on **Viale Regina Margherita, 12**, just a short walk from the Largo Carlo Felice tram stop. Cover is **€8**, and drinks run **€5–€10**. You'll find live jazz trios most nights, plus open-jam sessions on Wednesday and Friday. To get there, hop on bus **#9** to the "Regina Margherita" stop.

Plan for **Friday nights** when the full combo lineup takes the stage and the room buzzes with energy. Arrive early—seating is limited, and the best tables fill up fast. Why go? You'll hear authentic New York-style jazz right in the heart of Cagliari, complete with warm lighting and a friendly crowd.

2. Torre delle Stelle Music Hall

For a beachside concert, head to Torre delle Stelle. This open-air stage on Poetto Beach blends live music with sea views and summer breezes.

You'll find it at **Lungomare Poetto, 218**, a quick walk from the Poetto bus stop. Ticket prices range from **€10–€25**, depending on the act. The hall hosts indie rock bands, folk groups, and lively beach parties all summer long. To reach it, take bus **#8** to "Poetto," then stroll along the promenade.

The scene is at its best in **July and August**, when sunset concerts draw both locals and visitors. Bring a light scarf or jacket—the sea breeze cools off after dark. This venue stands out for its blend of music and nature: dancing under the stars with the sound of waves in the background.

3. Civic Theatre Loft Bar

Tucked inside the Civic Theatre, this loft-style bar is perfect for a relaxed evening of unplugged music and new voices.

Civic Theatre Loft Bar sits at **Via Roma, 145**, a short walk from the main Piazza Yenne. Cover charge is **€5**, and cocktails cost around **€7**. You'll find singer-songwriter nights and acoustic sessions most Thursdays from **21:00 to 23:00**. To get there, catch bus **#3** to the "Via Roma" stop.

Thursday nights are ideal, when local musicians take the mic in a warm, intimate setting. Small tapas plates (€4–€6) pair perfectly with a glass of wine as you listen. This spot is great if you want to discover rising Sardinian talent in a space where you can chat with artists between sets.

4. Sputnik Club

Ready to dance until dawn? Sputnik Club delivers cutting-edge electronic and techno beats in an industrial-style warehouse.

Find Sputnik at **Via Sardegna, 33**, near the train station. Entry is **€12**, and drinks cost **€6–€12**. Look for themed club nights and guest DJs spinning from **01:00 to 05:00**. The easiest way is by bus **#4** or **#7** to "Via Sardegna."

Saturday after-hours is when the crowd really shows up—young, energetic, and ready to dance. Before heading out, check Sputnik's Facebook page: they often post guest-list info for free entry before midnight. It's the spot for late-night energy, bold visuals, and a true taste of Cagliari's underground scene.

Cultural Centers and Creative Spaces

Cagliari's creative scene isn't limited to galleries and theatres. Scattered around the city you'll find former factories turned into hubs, leafy courtyards hosting tech talks, and cafés where art and conversation meet. These cultural centers and creative spaces are perfect for anyone who wants to see Cagliari's modern spirit in action.

1 Lanificio Cagliari

Lanificio Cagliari began life as a wool mill. Today it's a bright, open venue where art, design, and entrepreneurship come together.

Located at **Via San Domenico 22**, Lanificio opens free to the public. When special events roll in, tickets cost €5–€15. Here you can browse ongoing art residencies or stop by a design fair showcasing local makers. Startup meetups often fill the large ground-floor hall. Walk or ride bus **#6** to the "San Domenico" stop—it drops you right outside. If you can, visit on a **Creative Saturday** (once a month), when the full space opens for demos, talks, and a pop-up market. There's a small café on site that uses ingredients from Sardinian farms, so grab a coffee and a snack while you soak up ideas in the former mill's airy rooms.

2 Hub Villa Muscas

Tucked behind a line of plane trees, Hub Villa Muscas is Cagliari's answer to a modern innovation campus.

You'll find it at **Via Newton 10**. Community gatherings and film nights are free, but hands-on workshops run €10–€20. In the leafy courtyard you might catch a tech talk on smart-city projects or join an evening hackathon. To get here, take bus **#7** to the "Villa Muscas" stop and walk a few steps through the gate. Wednesdays bring a popular **Film & Pizza** night—movies start around 20:00, and pizza is €5 a slice. If you plan to linger or need a desk between events, monthly co-working passes are available. This blend of culture, tech, and local energy makes Villa Muscas a must-see for curious travelers.

3 Factory Café & Art Space

Factory Café is casual by design—a place for coffee, conversation, and creative sparks.

Head to **Via Ospedale 14**, a three-minute stroll from the "Ospedale Civile" bus stop on line **#5**. A simple espresso is €2; cappuccinos run €3. Most days, entry is free, though special events—like gallery openings or poetry slams—may ask for a small fee. On Sunday afternoons (15:00–18:00), local artists display paintings, photographs, and mixed media across the walls. On other nights you might find a board-game meetup or an open-mic poetry session. In May, Factory hosts a mini-art fair with up to 20 local artisans selling prints and handmade crafts. The relaxed vibe makes it easy to linger over your drink and discover fresh talent.

4 Spazio 29

Spazio 29 sits on a quiet corner of the Castello district—a cozy spot for dance, theatre, and photo exhibits.

You'll find it in **Piazza Carlo Alberto 29**, a short walk from either bus **#4** or **#14** ("Carlo Alberto" stop). Entry is free for most shows; masterclasses (dance or photography) cost about €20. Friday evenings bring lively improv theatre sessions starting at 20:30, where actors pull audience suggestions onstage. Daytime you may find a small photography exhibit or a community-led dance workshop. Because it sits in a shaded square, you can stop by any time to check the bulletin board for pop-up street performances. Sign up for their newsletter to hear about last-minute events—Spazio 29 always has something new to offer.

Chapter 7: Beaches and Waterfront Escapes

Poetto Beach

Poetto Beach is the most popular and accessible beach in Cagliari. It stretches for about 8 kilometers along the southeastern coast of the city and offers something for everyone—families, solo travelers, joggers, cyclists, swimmers, and those who just want to relax by the sea. It's not just a beach; it's a central part of daily life in Cagliari.

Address: Viale Poetto, 09126 Cagliari
Price: Free; parking costs around €1-2/hour
Activities: Swimming, beach volleyball, cycling, kitesurfing, paddleboarding, seaside dining

How to Get There:
Reaching Poetto is easy and affordable. If you're staying in the city center, the CTM public buses #1 or #5 from Piazza Matteotti take you directly to the beach area. The journey takes about 15-20 minutes depending on traffic. Buses run regularly, and tickets can be bought from kiosks or apps for around €1.30. If you're driving, just follow signs for "Poetto" or "Lido," and you'll find designated parking areas near the Lido di Elmas and Marina Piccola.

Best Time to Visit:
The best months to visit are from **late May to early September**, when the weather is warm and beach services are in full swing. If you want to avoid the crowds, go early in the morning (before 10:00 AM) or after 5:00 PM, especially in July and August. Sunset walks are also lovely here.

Why You Should Visit:
Poetto is a convenient escape within the city. Despite being so close to the urban area, the beach is clean, wide, and well-maintained. Locals use it not just for sunbathing but also for socializing and sports. I remember one early morning in

June when I walked along the shore with a coffee in hand. The air was fresh, joggers passed by, and the sea was completely still—like a sheet of glass. A few people were already out on paddleboards, and the only sounds were birds and soft waves. It's peaceful, even with the city just behind you.

AdditionalInfo:
There are beach bars (called *chioschi*) dotted along the promenade that serve drinks, snacks, and full meals—great for a casual lunch without leaving the beach. Near Lido di Quartu, you can often find **free rentals** for kayaks or stand-up paddleboards, especially on promotional days during the summer season. Lifeguards are stationed at regular intervals between **June and September**, adding a layer of safety for families and less experienced swimmers. There are also changing rooms, public toilets, and shaded benches available.

Calamosca Beach

If you're looking for a smaller, quieter beach away from the busy energy of Poetto, Calamosca is a perfect choice. This small cove is tucked between cliffs, offering clear water and a more intimate feel. It's ideal for travelers who want to escape the crowds without going far.

Address: Località Calamosca, 09126 Cagliari
Price: Free; limited parking available at €0.50/hour
Activities: Snorkeling, swimming, relaxing with a picnic, quiet reading

How to Get There:
Take **bus #8** from the city center. It departs from Via Roma and stops at the Calamosca terminus. From there, it's a short downhill walk (about 5 minutes) to reach the beach. If you drive, be aware that parking is limited, especially during weekends. Arrive early or be prepared to walk a bit from the upper parking area.

Best Time to Visit:
Visit during **June or September**. In June, the sea is warming up, and the cliffs offer natural shade during the late afternoon. In September, the weather is still pleasant, but most tourists have gone home, making the experience quieter and more relaxed.

Why You Should Visit:
Calamosca has a calm, peaceful atmosphere that feels very different from Cagliari's bigger beaches. The clear water and rocky bottom make it ideal for **snorkeling**. I once brought my snorkel gear in early June and ended up swimming alongside a school of bright blue damselfish near the rocks—an unexpected but amazing experience, especially just minutes from the city. It's also great for a picnic. Locals often bring sandwiches and soft drinks to enjoy while sitting on the rocks or under a shady tree.

Additional Info:
There are **no official facilities** at the beach, so plan accordingly. Bring your own water, snacks, and beach umbrella if needed. There's a small hotel and a simple restaurant nearby, but they're not always open outside peak season. The beach itself is a mix of sand and stone, so **water shoes** are recommended, especially if you plan to walk around the rocky edges or climb up the cliffs for a better view.

Mari Pintau

If you're looking for a beach that feels like a living postcard, Mari Pintau is the place. The name literally means "Painted Sea," and once you get there, it's easy to understand why. Located along the scenic SS125 coastal road, about a 30-minute drive from Cagliari, this spot is famous for its colorful, crystal-clear water that changes from emerald green to deep turquoise depending on the sunlight.

Address: SS125 km 12.5, 09045 Quartu Sant'Elena
Price: Free access; paid parking is available for about €1 per hour.

Mari Pintau is a rocky beach with pebbles rather than soft sand, so bringing water shoes is a smart idea. The beach itself is narrow and sits at the base of a steep slope, which you'll need to walk down from the roadside parking. There aren't any beach clubs, umbrellas, or lounge chairs, so you'll need to bring your own towel, shade, and snacks. That said, its wild beauty more than makes up for the lack of facilities.

Activities here are simple but memorable. Snorkeling is one of the top reasons people visit. The seabed is full of small rocks and seaweed patches that attract a variety of fish. On a clear day, which is often, you can easily spot them just a few meters from shore. I personally spent almost two hours floating and watching tiny silver fish dart between rocks. It's also a favorite spot for amateur photographers. The way the sun hits the water around 10 a.m. makes the entire bay shimmer. Even with just a smartphone, you'll walk away with stunning shots.

If you're an experienced swimmer, the deeper waters are refreshing and less crowded. However, the current can be strong, especially further out, so it's not ideal for small children or inexperienced swimmers. No lifeguards are on duty, so always use caution.

How to Get There:
The easiest way to get to Mari Pintau is by driving. Head northeast from Cagliari on the SS125, a beautiful coastal road with sea views. The drive alone is worth it. You'll find a few roadside parking areas near the beach—get there early, especially in July and August, as they fill up quickly. If you don't have a car, a seasonal shuttle bus operates in high summer (July–August) from Cagliari's main bus terminal to the nearby drop-off point.

Best Time to Visit:
Visit in the morning during summer, ideally before 10:30 a.m., to beat the crowds and catch the best lighting. July mornings are particularly calm and colorful. Weekdays are much quieter than weekends.

Why You Should Visit:
This beach stands out because of its colors and clarity. It's not your typical lounging beach, but rather a spot to sit quietly, take in nature, and enjoy the beauty of the Mediterranean at its purest. If you enjoy peaceful, undeveloped beaches with jaw-dropping views, Mari Pintau is well worth the trip.

Spiaggia di Solanas

Just over an hour's drive from Cagliari, **Spiaggia di Solanas** offers a long stretch of soft sand and a much more relaxed vibe than some of the region's better-known beaches. Tucked away in a small bay, it's the kind of place where you can truly unwind—whether you want to swim, enjoy a drink at a beach bar, or just lie back under an umbrella.

Address: Località Solanas, 09049 Sinnai
Price: Entry is free; sunbed and umbrella rentals cost around €3–5.

Solanas is a fairly wide beach with fine golden sand and clear shallow waters, making it ideal for families or anyone looking for an easy swimming spot. On windy days, you'll spot windsurfers gliding across the water—a local rental shack sometimes offers gear and short lessons. What I loved most during my visit was the laid-back, uncrowded feel. Even in summer, you can find a quiet corner to yourself, especially if you arrive before noon.

The beach is equipped with a few modest facilities. There are two beach bars (chioschi) where you can grab a cold drink, a sandwich, or even a full plate of pasta. Bathrooms and outdoor showers are available, but limited, so don't expect luxury. Bring your own supplies if you're staying for the day.

One summer evening, I happened upon a small pop-up reggae party right on the beach. A local DJ set up near the shoreline, and people danced barefoot on the sand as the sun dipped into the sea. It wasn't planned, and that's the magic of Solanas—it still feels spontaneous and personal.

How to Get There:
Driving is the most flexible option, especially if you want to stay for the sunset or explore nearby beaches. From Cagliari, head east on the SS125, and follow signs toward Solanas. There's a decent amount of parking, but during high season weekends, it may fill up by mid-morning.

If you don't have a car, your best bet is the **Trenino Verde**, a scenic tourist train that operates from Cagliari to Solanas on Sundays during the summer. It's slow, but the views are great. Taxis from Cagliari cost approximately €40–50 one way, which is practical for a group or family.

Best Time to Visit:
Late June to mid-August is perfect for a visit, when the beach bars are open and the weather is ideal. Weekdays are generally quieter, especially early mornings and after 5 p.m.

Why You Should Visit:
Solanas is great if you want a classic beach day without the noise and chaos of big resorts. It's accessible, scenic, and not overly developed. Whether you want to relax under an umbrella or join an impromptu beach party, Solanas gives you options without ever feeling crowded or commercial.

Punta Molentis

Punta Molentis is a picture-perfect beach located near the town of Villasimius, about an hour's drive from Cagliari. It's a small but scenic cove that combines soft sand, clear water, and striking rock formations, making it one of the most beautiful coastal spots in southern Sardinia. If you're looking for a quiet beach with postcard-worthy views, this is a must-visit.

Address: SP17, 09049 Villasimius (approx. 45 km from Cagliari)
Price: Free entry; parking costs €2-3 per hour during summer
Activities: Kayaking, snorkeling, photography, hiking nearby trails

How to Get There:
The best way to reach Punta Molentis is by car. From Cagliari, follow SP17 southeast through the scenic coast road toward Villasimius. Once you arrive near the beach, you'll see a designated parking area. From there, it's a 10-minute downhill walk to the cove. During the summer season, there's also a shuttle bus from Villasimius town center that costs about €5 round-trip.

Best Time to Visit:
The best months to visit are May and September. These months offer warm weather and fewer crowds compared to the high summer season. The water is still pleasant for swimming, and the surroundings are peaceful enough to enjoy the beach in a more relaxed setting.

What to Expect:
Punta Molentis is a small cove framed by rocky hills and gentle cliffs. The beach itself is narrow but very clean, with powdery white sand and incredibly clear, shallow water near the shore. The seabed is a mix of sand and rocks, which

makes it ideal for snorkeling. Many fish swim near the rocks, and it's easy to spot marine life even in shallow areas.

One of the best ways to explore this area is by kayak. If you rent a kayak nearby, you can paddle along the coastline and discover hidden caves and small inlets. On my last trip, I kayaked around the point and came across a small grotto that only a few locals seemed to know about. The entrance was partially hidden by rocks, and once inside, it was quiet and cool—a peaceful place to sit and just enjoy the sound of the water.

Why Visit:
The main reason to visit Punta Molentis is for the stunning views and the sense of calm you'll find there. It's a great choice if you want to avoid busier beaches like Poetto or Villasimius during peak season. The dramatic contrast of turquoise water against the white sand and gray rocks creates a unique landscape that feels untouched. It's also ideal for couples or solo travelers who enjoy nature, photography, or simply relaxing without too much noise.

Additional Info:
There are no lifeguards stationed at Punta Molentis, and because the cove opens to deeper water, currents can sometimes be strong, especially at the mouth. Confident swimmers will be fine, but it's not the best spot for very young children or weak swimmers. There are some basic beach services nearby, like umbrella rentals and a small food kiosk, but bring water, snacks, and sunscreen just in case. Shade is limited, so consider bringing a sun tent or beach umbrella if you plan to stay for a few hours.

Spiaggia di Nora

Spiaggia di Nora is not just a beach—it's a journey into Sardinia's past. Located near the town of Pula, this beach sits right next to the ancient ruins of the Roman city of Nora, offering a rare mix of seaside relaxation and cultural exploration. It's the perfect destination for travelers who want to combine a swim in the sea with a visit to one of the island's most significant archaeological sites.

Address: Via Nora, 09010 Pula (approx. 20 km southwest of Cagliari)
Price: Beach is free; entry to the archaeological site is €8 (includes museum access)
Activities: Swimming, sunbathing, touring ancient ruins, guided history tours

How to Get There:
You can easily reach Nora by taking a regional bus from Cagliari's Via Roma station. Buses depart about once every hour, and the ride to Pula takes roughly 40 minutes. From the Pula bus stop, it's a pleasant 10-minute walk along the coast to reach the beach and ruins. If you're driving, there's a small paid parking lot near the entrance.

Best Time to Visit:
The ideal times to go are in May and October, when the weather is warm but not too hot, and the tourist crowds are minimal. During these months, you can fully enjoy both the beach and the ruins at your own pace.

What to Expect:
Spiaggia di Nora has soft golden sand and calm, shallow water that makes it suitable for all ages. The beach is well-maintained and offers a few areas of natural shade from nearby trees. What makes it special, though, is its close proximity to the Roman ruins, which include an amphitheater, baths, mosaics, and ancient streets. The archaeological site is just a few steps from the beach, so you can explore the ruins in the morning and cool off with a swim in the afternoon.

On my last visit, I timed my walk through the ruins to end right around noon, just as the heat peaked. I made my way to the beach and slipped into the water for a quick swim. It was a surreal feeling—floating in the sea while looking back at stone arches and walls built two thousand years ago. That blend of history and nature is what makes Nora unforgettable.

Why Visit:
Nora is perfect for travelers who want more than just a day at the beach. It's a chance to connect with Sardinia's deep Roman roots while still enjoying the Mediterranean sunshine. Whether you're a history buff or just curious, visiting the ruins adds depth to the beach experience. It's also a very accessible destination, especially for those based in Cagliari.

Additional Info:
There are no major food options directly on the beach, but you'll find cafes and restaurants in nearby Pula. The archaeological site has no shade, so wear a hat and bring water if you plan to explore during midday. Guided tours are available in English and Italian, and they're worth joining if you want to learn the stories behind the ruins.

Tuerredda Beach

Tuerredda Beach is one of the most beautiful and popular beaches in southern Sardinia. Located between Chia and Teulada, this beach is known for its calm, crystal-clear water, fine white sand, and scenic surroundings. If you're looking for a relaxing beach day with a tropical feel, this is the perfect spot. Many locals compare it to the Caribbean—and it truly lives up to the hype.

Address: Località Tuerredda, 09010 Teulada (about 60 km south of Cagliari)
Price: Free access; sunbed and umbrella rental ranges from €5 to €10 per day. Parking costs around €3 per hour in the summer months.
Activities: Paddleboarding, swimming in shallow water, snorkeling, picnicking

Getting to Tuerredda is easiest by car. From Cagliari, it takes about 1 hour and 15 minutes. Drive along the scenic SP71 road from Teulada and watch for signs pointing to "Tuerredda." There's a parking area near the entrance, though it can fill up quickly during high season. If you don't have a car, a seasonal shuttle bus runs from Pula between mid-June and mid-September. A round-trip ticket costs about €10.

The best time to visit is early July. This is when the water is especially clear, and the Posidonia seagrass gives the sea a beautiful emerald-green tint. During peak summer (late July to mid-August), it gets very crowded, especially on weekends, so arriving early in the morning is recommended.

What makes Tuerredda stand out is the calm and shallow water, which makes it perfect for families with children and people who just want a gentle swim. Paddleboarding is a great option here because the waves are minimal, and you can see the seabed clearly as you float along. On one of my visits, I saw a family of loggerhead turtles swimming near the small island just off the beach—a moment I won't forget.

Facilities are available and well-maintained. There's a beach bar that offers simple but tasty food like bruschetta, sandwiches, and cold drinks. Toilets, outdoor showers, and changing rooms are also on-site.

Tuerredda Beach is ideal if you're looking for a peaceful escape with stunning views, soft sand, and calm waters. It's a place that stays with you long after your visit—simple, scenic, and soothing.

Chapter 8: Day Trips and Excursions from Cagliari

Nora Archaeological Park

If you're interested in history, sea views, and quiet surroundings, a trip to **Nora Archaeological Park** is one of the most rewarding day trips you can take from Cagliari. Nora, located just outside the small town of Pula, is considered one of Sardinia's oldest cities. This ancient site offers a unique combination of Roman ruins and coastal scenery, making it perfect for those who want to learn and relax at the same time.

Address: Via Nora, 09010 Pula CA
Entry Price: €5 for self-guided entry; guided tours range from €10-15 (recommended for better understanding)
How to Get There:
From Cagliari, take the **CTM bus 101** from Piazza Matteotti. A single ticket costs about €1.30, or you can get a day pass for €6.90. The journey by bus takes approximately one hour. Alternatively, if you're renting a car, it's a **40-minute drive** (around 40 km) along the SS195 coastal road, which offers nice views of the sea.

What to Do:
Once you arrive, you'll enter a well-preserved archaeological area where you can see the remains of a Roman amphitheater, ancient houses, mosaic floors, and the ruins of a temple. Many visitors start by walking through the **stone-paved streets** of the old Roman town. If you're on a guided tour, your guide will explain the meaning behind the mosaics and point out key landmarks like the public baths and the sanctuary. One of the most impressive sights is the **small Roman theater**, which still has seating areas and gives you a great view of the sea beyond.

Don't miss the spot where two different eras meet—the **Phoenician foundation stones** right below the later Roman structures. This part of the site helps you understand how old and layered this city truly is.

Best Time to Visit:
Plan to visit in **spring (April to June)** or early autumn (September), when the weather is warm but not too hot. The site is open year-round, but during summer, the lack of shade can make midday visits uncomfortable. Early mornings are ideal to avoid both heat and crowds.

Why You Should Visit:
This is one of Sardinia's best archaeological sites and a perfect place to experience ancient history in a peaceful, natural setting. Walking among the ruins while hearing the sound of the waves creates a calm and reflective experience. It's also not overly touristy, so you'll often find quiet corners where you can pause and imagine life as it was 2,000 years ago.

Additional Tips:
- Wear **comfortable walking shoes**, as some paths are uneven.
- There's **very little shade**, so bring a **hat, sunscreen, and plenty of water**, especially in summer.
- Public toilets and a small café are located near the ticket office.

If you're interested in local culture, consider combining your trip to Nora with a **walk through Pula town**, where you can enjoy local food and crafts. More on that in the next sections of the guide.

Villasimius & Porto Giunco

For travelers looking to escape the city and spend a relaxing day by the sea, **Villasimius** and its famous beach **Porto Giunco** make for a perfect day trip. This coastal area is known for its white sand beaches, shallow clear waters, and natural beauty. It's a favorite with locals and tourists alike who want to swim, snorkel, or simply unwind in a peaceful beach setting.

Address: SS18, 09049 Villasimius CA
Entry Price: Beach access is **free**, but during high season you might pay **€1–2 per hour for parking**.
How to Get There:
Take the **ARST bus 501** from **Largo Carlo Felice** in central Cagliari. The journey takes about **1 hour and 15 minutes**. Buses run a few times a day, especially in summer. If you prefer more flexibility, renting a car is a great option. The drive from Cagliari is about **60 km** along **SS554**, and while some sections are winding, the views of the coastline are worth it.

What to Do:
The highlight here is **Porto Giunco Beach**, known for its soft white sand and calm waters. It's ideal for swimming, especially for families with children due to the shallow shoreline. If you enjoy water sports, there are places to **rent snorkel gear, paddleboards**, and even **kayaks**.

Just behind the beach, you'll find a saltwater lagoon, home to **pink flamingos**, which can often be seen feeding or flying overhead. A short hike up to the **Torre di Porto Giunco**, a watchtower built centuries ago, offers a fantastic panoramic view of the coastline and the town below. The walk takes about **15–20 minutes** and is manageable even for casual walkers.

Best Time to Visit:
The best months to visit are **June to early September** when the sea is warm and the beach is in full swing. However, May and late September are great if you want to avoid the bigger summer crowds while still enjoying good weather.

Why You Should Visit:
Villasimius is one of Sardinia's most beautiful coastal areas. Even though it has become more popular in recent years, it still feels much more **relaxed and natural** than busier resorts on mainland Italy. You can enjoy a full day of beach fun, nature, and great food, all within easy reach of Cagliari.

Additional Tips:
- There are several **chiringuitos** (small beach bars) right on the sand. These serve **fresh seafood, salads, and cold drinks**. One highly

recommended spot is **Palmira Beach Café**, which serves grilled prawns and homemade granita.
- Parking can fill up fast by **mid-morning in summer**, so arrive early if you're driving.
- Public restrooms and changing areas are available, though basic.

If you want a peaceful end to your beach day, hang around for **sunset**, when the sky turns orange and the sea reflects shades of pink and gold. It's the perfect photo opportunity and a lovely way to wrap up a laid-back excursion.

Su Nuraxi di Barumini:

If you're curious about ancient civilizations and want to experience something truly unique to Sardinia, then a day trip to **Su Nuraxi di Barumini** is a must. Located in the quiet inland village of Barumini, this UNESCO World Heritage Site showcases the best example of a **nuraghe**—a mysterious stone tower built by the island's prehistoric Nuragic people. Visiting this site is not just about looking at ruins; it's about walking into the heart of Sardinia's deep, ancient past.

Address: SS293, 09040 Barumini SU
Price: €15 for adults, €12 for teens (13-17), €9 for children (7-12), free for kids under 6. The site can only be visited via guided tour.
How to Get There: If you're traveling by public transport, take the **ARST bus from Piazza Matteotti** in Cagliari. The ride takes about **2 hours** and passes through small towns. Driving is more convenient—just head north on **SS131**, then turn onto **SS293** toward Barumini. The total distance is around **55 kilometers**. There's free parking on-site.
Activities: The main attraction here is the **nuraghe tower complex**, built between 1600 and 1200 BCE. The tour lasts about **30-40 minutes** and takes you through narrow stone corridors, up spiral staircases, and inside the heart of the beehive-shaped towers. Guides explain how the towers were used for defense, community living, and rituals. You'll see massive stones perfectly placed without mortar—a true feat of engineering for the time.
After the tour, head across the road to the **Casa Zapata Museum**, a beautifully

restored Spanish-era mansion that was built directly on top of another nuraghe. Here, you'll get a top-down view of the ruins through glass floors, plus insight into the aristocratic life of Sardinia in past centuries. Entry is often included with the main ticket.

Best Time to Visit: Plan your trip between **April and October** when the site offers regular tours every **30 minutes**. Avoid midday in the summer—it gets very hot, and there's limited shade.

Why You Should Visit: Su Nuraxi isn't just a bunch of rocks—it's one of the best-preserved windows into Sardinia's ancient past. You don't need to be a history buff to enjoy this place. The scale of the construction, the mystery behind how and why these towers were built, and the stories shared by the guides make it easy to appreciate. You'll leave with a deeper respect for the island's culture.

Additional Info: If you have more time and a rental car, take a short **20-minute drive north to the Giara Plateau**. It's known for its open landscapes and wild **Giara horses**—small, semi-wild ponies that roam freely. It's a peaceful spot with great views, and perfect if you want to end your historical trip with a bit of nature.

Pula Town & Workshops:

Just a short drive southwest of Cagliari lies the welcoming town of **Pula**, a laid-back place full of charm, local flavor, and artisan traditions. While many travelers pass through here on the way to **Nora**, Pula is worth stopping for on its own. It's one of those towns where you can slow down, explore at your own pace, and truly feel the rhythm of Sardinian daily life.

Address: Piazza del Popolo, 09010 Pula CA
Price: Free to explore. Local artisan goods such as pottery, jewelry, and textiles range from **€10 to €30**, depending on what you buy.
How to Get There: The easiest way is to take the **same ARST bus (Line 129 or 130)** from Cagliari's **Piazza Matteotti**—it stops in Pula before reaching Nora. The ride takes around **45 minutes to 1 hour**. By car, drive west along **SS195** for about **35 kilometers**. Free and paid parking options are available in town.
Activities: Pula is known for its **traditional crafts**. You can visit small workshops

and stores where artisans create and sell **hand-painted ceramics**, **woven textiles**, and **red coral jewelry**, which is unique to Sardinia. Don't be shy—many shopkeepers are happy to show you how the items are made.

After shopping, take a seat in the main **Piazza del Popolo** and enjoy a **cappuccino or gelato** as you watch locals gather and kids play. If you're hungry, stop at a bakery and try **pane carasau**, Sardinia's famous crispbread, or pick up a **freshly made focaccia** from one of the old-school bakeries tucked into the side streets.

Best Time to Visit: Late afternoon is best. The heat of the day begins to fade, and most shops reopen after the mid-afternoon break (known as **riposo**, similar to siesta). In summer, the town hosts small music performances and food fairs in the square.

Why You Should Visit: Pula offers a gentle contrast to the busy beaches and archaeological sites nearby. It's a perfect example of Sardinia's small-town life—unhurried, friendly, and full of simple pleasures. Whether you want to pick up a handmade souvenir or just sip espresso under a tree, you'll find something memorable here.

Additional Info: One hidden treat is the **tiny pasticceria on Via Repubblica**, which makes **seadas**, a classic Sardinian dessert made of **fried pastry filled with cheese and drizzled with honey**. It's sweet, savory, and totally addictive. Ask for it fresh out of the fryer for the best experience.

Iglesias & Mining Heritage

A quiet and historical day trip, Iglesias takes you far from the beach crowds and into the heart of Sardinia's industrial and religious past. With its medieval center and mining heritage, this small town offers a different kind of charm, perfect for travelers curious about the island's less-touristy side.

Iglesias is located about 65 kilometers northwest of Cagliari, easily reachable by car in about 1 hour via the SS130, or by ARST bus in roughly 1 hour and 20 minutes. Despite its small size, the town has a rich and layered history. Once a thriving mining hub, it still retains a strong connection to its industrial roots, which you can explore through museums and nearby mine sites.

Begin your visit at **Piazza Municipio**, the town's central square, where you'll find the **Cathedral of Santa Chiara**. This Gothic church, dating back to the 13th century, is free to enter and sits peacefully at the heart of Iglesias. Its large bell tower and arched interiors give a quiet but impressive introduction to the town's medieval character.

Afterward, take time to explore the **Museo dell'Arte Mineraria**, a small but fascinating mining museum located inside an old school building. For just €3–5, visitors can walk through original mining equipment, helmets, lamps, and educational exhibits that explain what daily life was like for miners in the 19th and 20th centuries. The real draw is the guided underground tunnel simulation, where former miners and guides walk you through what working inside Sardinian mines felt like. It's a hands-on, immersive experience—especially engaging if you're traveling with older kids or anyone interested in engineering or history.

A real tip here is to **ask about guided excursions to the Monteponi and Porto Flavia mine sites**, which lie just outside town. Though not always advertised, local guides can arrange visits to old shafts, tunnels, and even sea-facing loading docks that were once engineering marvels. These tours usually cost around €10–15 and provide a powerful glimpse into how vital mining was to Sardinia's economy.

Strolling through Iglesias' backstreets is also a pleasure. You'll find pastel-colored houses, quiet piazzas, and small cafés where locals sip coffee in the afternoon sun. It's not flashy, but that's part of the appeal. It feels real and lived-in, with an old-world vibe that's hard to fake.

Best time to visit? Spring or autumn is ideal. The temperatures are mild—usually around 20°C—and the streets are calm and easy to explore on foot. Summer can be hot, and many locals head to the coast, so shops may keep shorter hours.

If you're looking for a quieter, more reflective experience beyond the beaches and tourist zones, Iglesias delivers. It tells a story of Sardinia that's not often heard— one of miners, craftsmen, and centuries of history hidden in stone and dust.

Costa Rei Beach

If you're craving a relaxing day by the sea, Costa Rei offers one of the most beautiful and peaceful beaches near Cagliari. It's a favorite among locals for good reason—wide sandy stretches, shallow waters, and a calm vibe make this spot perfect for a quiet beach escape.

Located about 70 kilometers southeast of Cagliari, Costa Rei is easy to reach by car via SS554 and SS125. The drive takes around 1 hour and 15 minutes. If you don't have a car, the **ARST bus 501** also continues from Villasimius and reaches Costa Rei in about 1 hour and 45 minutes in total. It's a bit of a trip, but the peaceful shoreline makes the journey worth it.

The beach itself stretches for several kilometers. It's known for its **fine golden sand and clear, shallow water**, making it ideal for families with children or anyone looking to swim and relax. The sea here is calm and safe, especially in the summer months, and lifeguards are often on duty at the more popular spots.

You can **rent sunbeds and umbrellas** on site for around €5-10 per day, or simply bring a towel and find your own space—it's rarely too crowded, even during peak season. There are also **kayaks and paddleboards** available for rent if you're feeling more active. One of the highlights is paddling along the coast toward the nearby rocks and cliffs, which offer a more scenic view of the bay and some great photo opportunities.

A favorite stop for many is the **beachfront café at the southern end of Costa Rei**, where you can grab a cold drink, order a simple panini, or try some local gelato. It's the perfect break between swims or to just sit back and enjoy the sea breeze.

When to go? The best time to visit Costa Rei is from **July through mid-September**, when the sea is warmest and most inviting. That said, June and late September also offer great weather with fewer visitors, so they're perfect for travelers who prefer a quieter atmosphere.

It's a good idea to pack your own snacks and water if you plan to stay all day, as some stretches of the beach are more isolated. That's also part of the charm—this beach isn't overdeveloped. It feels natural and spacious, with plenty of room to stretch out and enjoy the sound of waves.

Costa Rei is all about simplicity. No big attractions, no noise—just clear water, soft sand, and a peaceful setting. If you're looking to recharge away from the busier beaches closer to Cagliari, this is where you'll want to go.

Barumini + Nora Combined Excursion

If you're eager to dive deep into Sardinia's rich history in just one day, combining **Su Nuraxi in Barumini** and the **ancient ruins of Nora** makes for an unforgettable experience. This day trip is perfect for travelers who want a blend of prehistoric architecture and coastal Roman ruins, all within a short drive from Cagliari. While the two sites are very different, together they offer a complete picture of Sardinia's long and layered past.

Why It Works:
Start your morning in **Barumini**, home to **Su Nuraxi**, a UNESCO World Heritage Site. These ancient stone towers—called nuraghe—were built by Sardinia's mysterious Nuragic civilization around 3,500 years ago. A guided tour (included in the entry fee) leads you through narrow stone corridors and lookout towers. It's a short but fascinating visit that typically lasts under an hour. After your visit, you can explore the nearby **Casa Zapata Museum**, which displays artifacts and offers a glass-floor view of another nuraghe below the building.

Next, hop back into your car and head south toward **Nora**, just outside the town of **Pula**. The drive takes about 1 hour and 15 minutes (roughly 70 km) through peaceful countryside and coastal roads. Nora is Sardinia's oldest city and was once a thriving Phoenician and later Roman settlement. Here, you can walk through the remains of a Roman theater, mosaicked houses, and ancient baths— all right by the sea. The ruins are atmospheric, especially in the late afternoon when the sun starts to drop and the sea breeze picks up.

Transport Tip:
The easiest way to make this combined trip is by **renting a car** (around €60 per day). It gives you full control of your schedule and allows you to move between

the two locations comfortably. If you prefer not to drive, some **local tour companies offer private shuttle options**, though they are more expensive.

What to Pack:
Bring **sturdy walking shoes**, as the ground at both sites is uneven. Pack **picnic snacks**, water, sunscreen, and a **camera**, especially for Nora, where the sea backdrop makes for great photos.

Best Time to Go:
The **shoulder seasons**—May or September—are ideal. It's cooler, less crowded, and both sites operate regular guided tours during these months.

Additional Info:
Before heading back to Cagliari, consider a **short detour to Santa Gilla Lagoon**, located just outside the city. This peaceful spot is home to **flamingos** and other birdlife and makes a calm and scenic end to your day of historical exploration.

Chapter 9: Shopping and Local Products

Via Manno and Via Garibaldi

These two parallel streets form Cagliari's style hub. Along Via Manno and Via Garibaldi, you'll find a mix of high-end labels, eco-friendly workshops, and up-and-coming designers. Whether you're hunting for a statement piece or a simple accessory, this area delivers a fun, relaxed shopping stroll. Here's a closer look at five spots you won't want to miss.

Luigi Mura Boutique

Located at Via Manno 25, Luigi Mura is a small shop with big personality. Inside, racks of linen shirts, lightweight trousers, and breezy dresses catch your eye. Prices run from about €80 to €250, which feels fair for pieces that blend classic Italian tailoring with Mediterranean flair. Plan to arrive between 10 am and noon—the natural light in the airy showroom makes fabrics glow. Take bus 3 to the "Via Manno" stop, then stroll up the gentle hill. The staff here love custom requests: ask for a pop of color on a trim or a tweak to a hem, and they'll arrange it. It's the perfect spot for polished vacation wear that doubles as everyday staples back home.

Blumarine Outlet

Just around the corner at Via Garibaldi 68, Blumarine Outlet is your go-to for discounted designer finds. Sale racks hold last-season jackets, skirts, and blouses priced from €50 to €150. If you time it right—Monday afternoons after weekend restocks—you'll score the best selection. To get there, hop on tram line T2 to "Giardini Pubblici," then walk three minutes. Beyond the bargains, chatting with the friendly staff is part of the experience: they'll clue you in on upcoming drops or help you piece together an outfit. It feels like snagging a Milan runway look without the usual price tag.

Sardegna Style

Eco-conscious shoppers will love Sardegna Style at Via Manno 42. Here, cork handbags, hand-printed silk scarves, and other unique accessories range from €30 to €90. The shop doubles as a mini-workshop, so you can watch artisans demonstrate how they turn raw cork into soft, wearable bags. It's easy to reach on foot—just a ten-minute walk from Piazza Yenne. Drop by in the early afternoon, when artisans are most likely in the store. You'll leave not only with a stylish souvenir but also a new appreciation for Sardinia's eco-friendly materials.

Boutique Oltre

Tucked into Via Garibaldi 102, Boutique Oltre spotlights minimalist labels by Sardinian designers. Dresses, tops, and trousers here cost between €60 and €200. Weekday mornings are ideal, since you'll often have the place to yourself, along with one-on-one styling help. Just take bus 5 to the "Galleria Civica" stop and walk two minutes. If you're curious about local talent, this is where you'll find it before it hits the wider Italian fashion scene. Their fitting rooms have full-length mirrors and gentle lighting, so you can really imagine each look in your own closet.

Moda Castello

Moda Castello at Via Sant'Avendrace 18 feels like a secret garden. This courtyard-front shop focuses on casual-chic linen trousers, tunics, and breezy button-downs priced €40–€120. From the Bastione di Saint Remy viewpoint, it's an easy seven-minute downhill walk along Via Manno. Late afternoon visits bring soft light through the courtyard, making it a lovely backdrop for outfit selfies. The team here is laid-back but passionate: they'll suggest color pairings or styling tricks that highlight Cagliari's relaxed coastal vibe. It's the perfect spot to find a go-anywhere piece you'll love packing for beach days and city evenings alike.

Sardinian Jewelry and Coral Pieces

Cagliari's jewelry shops are more than stores—they're windows into Sardinia's past and present. Coral has been prized here for centuries, and local artisans turn it into pieces you'll treasure. Whether you're curious about how coral is harvested, want to see master silversmiths at work, or just find a wearable reminder of the island, this section will guide you through five top spots. Here's what to expect, how to get there, and why each is worth your time.

1. Corallo Arte
Just steps from the marina, Corallo Arte lets you see sustainable coral harvesting up close. As you enter, master jewelers might be carving raw coral into beads or polishing finished necklaces. You can ask them about the Gulf of Cagliari's harvest methods—strictly controlled to protect marine life—and then choose a classic red coral necklace to take home. Prices range from €70 to €400 based on size. Take Bus 7 to the "Via Baylle" stop; it's a one-minute walk. Visit in the morning to catch the jewelers at work and learn the real story behind each piece.

2. Gioielli di Nuraghe
At Piazza Garibaldi 5, Gioielli di Nuraghe blends Sardinia's ancient nuragic symbols with modern silverwork. When you arrive—tram T1 to "Piazza Yenne" plus a four-minute walk—you might see a silversmith engraving a spiral motif or crafting a pendant inspired by Bronze Age towers. Prices start at €120 and go up to €600 for silver-and-coral combos. Drop by in the early afternoon during live engraving demos. If you like a design, you can order a custom engraving to make the piece truly yours.

3. Sardegna in Oro
On Via Roma 56, Sardegna in Oro offers a sleek showroom of coral-set earrings, brooches, and rings. Take metro line M to "Cagliari Centro" and walk two minutes. On weekends, guest artisans join in, so you can hear talks on coral preservation and see different setting techniques. Pieces cost between €90 and €500. You'll find modern designs that still honor tradition. If sustainability matters to you, this is a must-visit: each item comes with information on how the coral was harvested and why preserving the reef matters.

4. Corallo Rosa
Corallo Rosa specializes in pink coral—a rare find in Cagliari. From the Marina, stroll along Via Roma for about ten minutes until you reach Via Sant'Efisio 10. Inside, you'll see pink-hued necklaces, bracelets, and rings displayed against soft lighting. Prices range from €80 to €300. Mid-morning visits let you join their

coral-dyeing demo, where artisans show how raw coral is treated to enhance its natural shade. This shop is the only one in town devoted entirely to pink coral, making it a unique stop for collectors and gift-givers alike.

5. Isola del Gioiello

Just off Via Garibaldi at number 12, Isola del Gioiello invites you to play mix-and-match with coral and local gemstones. Hop on Bus 4, get off at the "Via Garibaldi" stop, and it's a two-minute walk. Inside, tables are set up with trays of red and pink coral next to Sardinian agate, jasper, and more. Prices run from €100 to €550. Late afternoon is ideal—sunset light streams through the windows, making the coral glow. Knowledgeable staff will explain how gems are mined on nearby islands and help you pair them for a custom look.

Local Food Souvenirs:

Before you leave Cagliari, take home a taste of Sardinia. In this section, we'll explore five spots where you can sample—and buy—authentic cheese, wine, and the famed bottarga. Each place brings its own story, so you'll return with souvenirs that carry real local flavor.

1. Caseificio Podda

Nestled just outside town, Caseificio Podda is more than a shop—it's a working dairy where you can see cheese being made from start to finish.

At **Via Lungosaline 3**, you'll find fresh wheels of **fiore sardo**, **casu marzu**, and **pecorino**. Slices cost between **€5 and €12**. Between **9–11 am**, the cheese is at its freshest, so arrive early. Watch the cheese curds being pressed, then taste samples straight off the wheel. A taxi from the city center takes about 10 minutes, or catch bus 15 to "Lungosaline." This farm is one of the few in the EU still producing **casu marzu** under regulation—definitely a souvenir to brag about.

2. Enoteca Gatti

For wine lovers, Enoteca Gatti feels like visiting a Sardinian family's cellar.

You'll find them at **Piazza San Domenico 8**, with bottles priced **€8–€25**. Drop by for tastings in the **3–6 pm** window, when the friendly sommeliers open up new vintages of **cannonau** and **vermentino**. They can recommend bottles that ship easily, so you can send a case home. To get there, take tram T2 to "Giardini," then walk five minutes through a quiet square. It's worth it for the warm welcome and insider tips on pairing Sardinian wines with local dishes.

3. Bottega del Bottarga

This shop is dedicated to bottarga, the cured fish roe that Sardinia is famous for.

Head to **Via della Marina 22** to browse **100 g tins** priced **€30–€80**. In the **morning**, when fishermen unload their catch at the nearby harbor, the bottarga arrives fresh. You can watch the sun-drying process through a small window, then sample thin slivers on crisp crostini. It's just an **8-minute walk** from Marina Piccola beach. Bottarga here follows recipes that are centuries old, making it a must-buy for anyone who loves bold, salty flavors.

4. Mercato di San Benedetto

No trip to Cagliari is complete without a visit to Europe's largest covered fish market, paired with top local foods.

Find it at **Via San Benedetto 23**, where stalls run the gamut from fresh fish to **cheeses (€3–€15)**, **olive oils**, and **cured meats**. Arrive on a **weekday between 8–10 am** to beat the crowds and see the best picks. Bus 17 stops right outside the entrance. Wander the aisles, chat with vendors about their olive harvest or cheese affinage, and pick up picnic supplies or gift boxes. It's a sensory feast and a great way to stock up on edible souvenirs.

5. Cantina Lilliu

For a cozy, family-run wine experience, Cantina Lilliu is hard to beat.

Located at **Via Is Mirrionis 45**, bottles cost **€5–€20**. The small cellar tour takes you through barrels of **muscat** and local liqueurs, ending with a tasting under soft, late-afternoon light. To get there, take bus 9 to "Is Mirrionis," then walk three minutes. You'll hear stories of recipes passed down through generations. Whether you buy a single bottle or a mixed case, you'll leave feeling like part of the Lilliu family—and with a taste of Sardinia to share.

Traditional Handwoven Textiles and Rugs

Before you dive into Cagliari's bustling markets and boutiques, set aside a morning to explore the age-old craft of Sardinian weaving. Textiles here aren't just home goods—they're a link to the island's past. From the bright wool rugs of Orgosolo to the fine linen runners at La Tela di Sardegna, each workshop tells a story through color, pattern, and technique. Below are five spots where you can meet the makers, see looms in action, and carry home a piece of island heritage.

1. Tessitura Sarda Artigiana

Step into a small workshop tucked on Via Logudoro, and you'll find rows of wooden looms clacking all day. At **Tessitura Sarda Artigiana**, women and men guide shuttle after shuttle of wool yarn across the loom, creating bold, traditional motifs known as Su Marmuri patterns. You can watch them at work, feel the thick, hand-spun wool, and choose a table runner or small rug priced between €50 and €200. It's easiest to take a taxi from the city center—a 12-minute ride that saves you a steep uphill walk. Plan to arrive in the weekday morning hours when demo sessions are in full swing. Seeing these craftsmen at work shows you how much effort goes into each vibrant piece.

2. Ricami di Nonna

Not far from Piazza Costituzione, **Ricami di Nonna** offers a softer side of Sardinian craft. Here, delicate linens and tablecloths bear fine, hand-stitched patterns passed down through generations. Prices range from €20 for a small napkin to €80 for a full tablecloth. If you visit in the early afternoon—when their stitching workshops run—you can pick up a needle yourself and learn simple embroidery stitches from local artisans. Catch bus 12 to "Costituzione" and walk a block to the shop. Beyond shopping, you leave with a small keepsake you helped stitch, making the gift even more personal.

3. Filandari Textiles

Around the corner on Via Savoia, **Filandari Textiles** brings together alpaca-blend scarves and natural dyes from Sardinian plants. Scarves and shawls cost between €30 and €150. During weekday mornings, dyers mix colors from pomegranate skins, walnut husks, and local flowers, then show you how they soak yarn in vats of pigment. Take metro line M to "Monte Claro" and walk five minutes. A chat with the dyers helps you understand why each shade is tied to the island's landscape. These soft scarves make cozy souvenirs, and knowing how they're made adds a special touch.

4. La Tela di Sardegna

If fine linen is more your style, head to **La Tela di Sardegna** on Via Sonnino. Their cloth is woven from flax grown in Sardinia's fields, creating runners that feel cool to the touch. Prices fall between €40 and €120. You can run your hand over the even weave and hear stories of flax harvesting on the island's farms. Bus 16 to "Sonnino" drops you right outside. Mid-morning visits are best, as staff share "storytelling sessions" about how flax goes from seed to fabric. These linens are rare finds abroad, and they hold a piece of Sardinia's rural traditions.

5. Orgosolo Rugs

On Via Baylle, **Orgosolo Rugs** brings bright, geometric rugs inspired by the mountain village of Orgosolo. Hand-loomed by local weavers, these pieces range from €100 to €350 for small to medium sizes. To get there, take bus 7 to the "Via Baylle" stop and walk four minutes. Late mornings are ideal; all designs are on display, and you can learn about proper care for wool rugs—like gentle shaking and spot cleaning. The bold shapes and colors echo the island's rugged interior, making these rugs standout decor and a lasting reminder of Sardinian artistry.

Artisan Markets in Castello and Villanova

Cagliari's Castello and Villanova quarters come alive on market days. You'll find makers showing their work right on the street—pots, prints, upcycled clothes, even local treats. These markets offer a chance to meet artisans, watch them craft, and bring home something truly unique. Here's a closer look at the five best markets in these historic neighborhoods.

1. Mercatino di Castello

Start your Sunday with a stroll through this monthly market tucked inside the old city walls. Small stalls line Piazza Arsenale, offering hand-painted ceramics, leather wallets, and icons on wood panels. Prices run from about **€5 to €50**, so you can pick up both tiny trinkets and statement pieces. To get there, take the funicular from the Marina up to Castello—then it's a two-minute walk. The best time is the **first Sunday of each month** from **9 am to 2 pm**, when a rotating group of makers sets up shop. Go for the historic vibe: the market sits among medieval ramparts, making each find feel like part of Cagliari's past.

2. Villanova Vintage Fair

If you love reworked fashion, this once-a-month fair is for you. Held on **Via dei Genovesi** in Villanova, prices range **€10 to €80** for vintage scarves, upcycled denim, and printed silks. Hop on **Bus 6** to the "Villanova" stop and walk five minutes through narrow streets. The fair runs on the **last Saturday of every month**, from **10 am to 4 pm**, so plan for a midday visit. You'll pick up one-of-a-kind pieces—old Sardinian shawls remade into modern wraps, or retro dresses refashioned by local sewers. It's a blend of sustainability and style that you won't find in regular shops.

3. Artigiani in Piazza

Every Saturday morning, artisans set up in **Piazza San Sepolcro** to show live demos of pottery, wood carving, and printmaking. Items go for **€8 to €60**, with small bowls, carved spoons, and limited-run art prints. You can walk down from Bastione di Saint Remy in about ten minutes (it's mostly downhill) or take a quick taxi. The market is open **9 am to 1 pm** on Saturdays. Watch a potter throw clay on the wheel, then chat about glazing techniques. It's lively, hands-on, and a great way to see how local crafts come to life.

4. Notte Bianca Artisan Pop-Up

Once every quarter, Castello's narrow lanes fill with late-night pop-ups. You'll sip a glass of Sardinian wine while browsing jewelry, mini paintings, and handmade candles. Items cost **€15 to €75**. No transport needed—just wander on foot through the pedestrian-only streets. The event runs **7 pm to midnight**, usually in spring and autumn. The mix of soft street lighting and quiet alleys creates a relaxed festivity. It's a chance to shop under the stars and support artisans who take part in Cagliari's creative scene.

5. Mercato del Gusto Cagliari

On Sunday mornings, head to **Via Santa Croce 12** in Villanova for this combined food-and-crafts market. You'll pay **€5 to €30** for small jars of honey, local jams, plus soaps and hand-poured candles. Catch **Bus 14** to the "Santa Croce" stop, then walk two minutes. The market runs **8 am to 12 pm** on Sundays. Sample a spoonful of wildflower honey, then pick up a scented bar of lavender soap. This market stands out because you get edible treats alongside home goods—perfect for putting together a gift basket that's all Sardinian.

Bookstores, Art Shops, and Independent Makers

When you need a break from sightseeing, Cagliari's small galleries and bookshops offer a fresh change of pace. These spots aren't just stores—they're creative hubs where you can meet local artists, stumble on hidden stories, and take home something truly personal. Here are five must-visit places that capture Sardinia's artistic spirit.

1. Libreria Dessì

Nestled on a quiet side street, Libreria Dessì feels like a neighbor's living room turned bookstore. Step inside and you'll find shelves packed with Sardinian novels, local history, and travel guides that go deeper than any tourist brochure.

What You'll Do: Spend an hour browsing titles in Italian and English. In the late afternoon, settle in for a free reading or chat with an author over coffee.
Practical Tips: Take bus 2 to the "Via Sulis" stop, then walk two minutes. Books cost €10–€35. Visit around 5 pm to catch readings and informal meet-and-greets.
Why You'll Love It: You'll hear stories straight from local writers and leave with insights you won't find online.

2. Spazio Blanco

Housed in a bright space near Piazza Yenne, Spazio Blanco shows the work of up-and-coming Sardinian painters and printmakers. The gallery changes its line-up every month, so there's always something new to see.

What You'll Do: Explore the latest show, ask the curator about each piece, and pick up a limited-edition print.
Practical Tips: Walk eight minutes from Piazza Yenne along Via Manno. Prints and small paintings run €15–€80. Aim for the first Friday of the month, from 6–9 pm, when openings include light refreshments.
Why You'll Love It: You'll get a sneak peek at artists before they hit bigger galleries elsewhere.

3. Officina Creativa

Officina Creativa feels more like a workshop than a shop. Long tables hold stacks of blank journals and piles of colorful papers. You can join a quick DIY session or simply stock up on unique stationery.

What You'll Do: Make your own notebook with leather covers, hand-stitched bindings, and Sardinian-patterned papers.
Practical Tips: Take bus 8 to "Via Liguria." Materials cost €20–€60. Drop in on a Saturday or Sunday afternoon when staff run short 30-minute workshops.
Why You'll Love It: You'll walk out with a one-of-a-kind journal and a fun story about how you made it.

4. Il Gallo Nero

Tucked off Via Sassari, Il Gallo Nero focuses on hand-blown glassware and handcrafted pottery. Watching artisans at their furnace-hot kilns is a highlight.

What You'll Do: Observe a live glass-blowing demo, then choose colorful bowls or vases for your home.
Practical Tips: Catch a taxi or hop on bus 4 to "Via Sassari." Pieces range from €10–€50. Plan your visit for mid-morning (10–11 am) when demos run.
Why You'll Love It: Seeing molten glass transform into elegant shapes is both surprising and inspiring.

5. Merceria delle Idee

Merceria delle Idee is a treasure trove of beads, ribbons, and textiles. It's part craft store, part community center—where locals and visitors share ideas over a worktable.

What You'll Do: Pick out Sardinian-printed fabrics, colorful beads, and wood-block stamps. Join a free drop-in session to make a simple keychain or brooch.
Practical Tips: Bus 16 to "Via Sardegna" drops you right outside. Supplies run €5–€40. Afternoons are best when regular crafters gather.
Why You'll Love It: You can walk away with a handmade token or start a new hobby inspired by local techniques.

Sustainable and Eco-Friendly Shopping in Cagliari

Cagliari's green shops prove that shopping can be good for you and the planet. Whether you need a travel-friendly swap, an upcycled bag, or farm-fresh produce, these five spots make it easy to shop with purpose.

1. EcoCagliari Shop

Start your zero-waste journey here.
Located on Via Mameli 14, EcoCagliari stocks bamboo utensils, reusable bags, beeswax wraps, and more. Prices range from €3 for a set of bamboo straws up to €25 for a full zero-waste kit. Inside, local "eco-experts" explain simple swaps—like swapping plastic snack bags for cloth pouches. To get there, hop Bus 10 to the "Via Mameli" stop. Mornings are best: the store is quieter, and you'll have time to ask questions. It's worth a stop to pick up items that cut single-use plastics out of your trip and serve you afterward.

2. Sardinia Recycled

Find fashion that's kind to the earth.
At Via Fermi 22, this small workshop turns old fabric, plastic, and metal into tote bags, jewelry, and home décor. Prices run €10–€70, depending on size and detail.

You can watch founders at work—mid-day is prime time—to see how they transform waste into art. Take Bus 18 to "Via Fermi," then follow the sound of sewing machines. Buying here means you're supporting local upcycling and reducing landfill. Plus, each piece is one-of-a-kind, so you get a souvenir no one else has.

3. Green Living Cagliari

Natural self-care crafted locally.
Piazza del Carmine 4 houses shelves of organic soaps, lotions, and candles made with Sardinian herbs. Expect to pay €5–€30 for travel-size bars or small candles. In the afternoon, staff demo soap-making, showing you how they use lavender, rosemary, and myrtle. Take Tram T1 to the "Carmine" stop and follow the plaza signs. You'll leave with clean-ingredient essentials that are gentle on your skin and kind to local farms.

4. BioMarket Santa Gilla

Fill your bag with farm-fresh produce.
Every Saturday, local organic farmers gather at Via del Fangario 11, about a 15-minute taxi ride from the city center. Prices start at €2 for seasonal fruits and go up to €20 for specialty items like heirloom tomatoes or wild greens. The market runs 8 am–12 pm—arrive early to get the best pick. Chat directly with growers about their practices, then pack a picnic or bring ingredients back to your kitchen. This is the spot to taste Sardinia's true flavors straight from the source.

5. Fattoria Urbana

Green souvenirs that keep growing.
On Sunday mornings (9 am–1 pm), pop-up stalls line the Poetto promenade with potted herbs and small plants. Prices are €4–€15 for rosemary, basil, mint, and more. You can walk from any point along the beach, following signs for "Fattoria Urbana." Beyond shopping, you'll learn basic urban-gardening tips—perfect for taking home a living memory of Cagliari. A few sunny pots on your windowsill can remind you daily of sea breezes and salt air.

Chapter 10: Practical Information and Travel Tips

How to Get to Cagliari:

Getting to Cagliari is quite easy, whether you're flying in, arriving by ferry, or exploring other towns on the island. Here's what you need to know before your trip begins.

Most visitors arrive in Cagliari by plane. The city is served by **Cagliari Elmas Airport (CAG)**, located just 7 kilometers from the city center. It's the main airport for southern Sardinia and is well connected to major Italian cities like Rome, Milan, and Naples. You'll also find seasonal flights from other European countries, especially during the summer months, with budget airlines like **easyJet**, **Ryanair**, and **Volotea**, as well as national carriers like **ITA Airways**.

Once you land, getting into the city is quick and simple. The most convenient and affordable option is the **ARST shuttle train**, which runs roughly every 20 to 30 minutes and drops you at **Piazza Matteotti** (right in the center of town) in about 7 minutes. Tickets cost only **€1.30**, and you can buy them at the airport station or online. Trains are modern and reliable, making this an easy choice for travelers with light luggage.

If you're carrying heavier bags or arriving late at night, taxis are also available just outside the terminal. A taxi ride into central Cagliari will cost around **€20-€25**, and the journey takes about 10-15 minutes. Ride-sharing apps like Free Now may also operate depending on the season.

If you're traveling from mainland Italy and prefer not to fly, **ferries** are another option. **Porto di Cagliari** is the city's main ferry port, located close to the center. Companies such as **Grimaldi Lines** and **Tirrenia** operate regular routes from **Genoa**, **Naples**, and **Palermo**, often with overnight sailings. These ferries are comfortable and can accommodate both foot passengers and vehicles. It's best to **book in advance**, especially during summer and holidays, when crossings fill up quickly. Once docked, you're only a short walk or a **10-minute CTM bus ride** (lines 1 or 5) from the historic Castello district.

For travel within Sardinia, Cagliari is a central hub for **regional train services**. While there's **no rail connection to mainland Italy**, the island has a small but functional network operated by **Trenitalia**. From **Cagliari Centrale**, you can catch direct trains to towns like **Oristano, Iglesias, Carbonia**, and **San Gavino**. Tickets for these routes start at around **€5-€10**, depending on distance. The trains are clean and fairly punctual, though not especially fast, making them a good option for day trips or slow travel. Tickets can be purchased at the station kiosks, Trenitalia ticket offices, or online through their website and app.

If you prefer more flexibility, **car rentals** are widely available both at the airport and in the city. Driving in Cagliari is manageable, though parking in the historic areas can be tricky. If you plan to explore remote beaches or countryside locations, a rental car can be a smart investment.

Navigating the City:

Cagliari is a great city to explore on foot, but when you need to get around a bit quicker, local buses and the metro make public transportation easy and affordable.

One of the best things about Cagliari is that many of its main sights are close together. Districts like **Castello, Marina, Villanova**, and **Stampace** are all walkable and full of life. Cobblestone streets wind through colorful buildings, and you'll often find locals sitting at outdoor cafés or chatting in the piazzas. If you're up for walking, exploring on foot is both enjoyable and efficient. Just wear **comfortable shoes**, as some areas (like Castello) have steep hills and uneven pavements.

For longer distances, Cagliari has a reliable **public bus network** operated by **CTM** (Consorzio Trasporti e Mobilità). The buses are clean, modern, and fairly easy to use, even for non-Italians. A **single ticket costs €1.30** and is valid for **90 minutes** from the time of first use. You can buy tickets at **tobacconists (tabacchi)**, **newsstands**, vending machines at major bus stops, or digitally through the **Muver app**, which is available in English.

Bus stops display route numbers and schedules. During the day, buses generally run every **10 to 20 minutes**, depending on the line and time. Lines **1, 5, and 30** are among the most commonly used by visitors, serving central and residential areas. Most buses also have **digital signs** and **automated announcements** to tell you the next stop, which makes it easier for non-locals to navigate.

Cagliari also has a **light metro line**, known locally as the **Metrocagliari**. It's more like a tram or suburban train than a full metro system, but it's still useful for reaching neighborhoods like **Monserrato** and **Piazza Repubblica**, or connecting to **Elmas Airport**. The **same CTM ticket** works for both the metro and buses, making it easy to switch between them without extra cost.

If you're looking for a more active or eco-friendly way to get around, **bike and e-scooter rentals** are increasingly popular, especially in the warmer months. There are **bike lanes** along the **Poetto waterfront**, and companies like **RideMovi** or **Bit Mobility** allow you to rent scooters or bikes through an app. These are great for short rides between neighborhoods or just cruising by the beach. Helmets are recommended (and often required) when using e-scooters.

Taxis are available throughout the city, though they're not as common as in larger cities like Rome or Milan. You can find them at **designated taxi ranks** near bus stations, the airport, and large squares. Fares are metered, and short trips within the city usually cost €10–€15. For convenience, you can also book taxis via apps like **Free Now** or call one of the local taxi services.

Overall, Cagliari's size and layout make it easy to get around, whether you prefer to walk, take the bus, ride a bike, or hop in a taxi. Just remember to validate your ticket once you board any public transport and check operating hours, especially on **Sundays or public holidays**, when service may be reduced.

Cost Breakdown:

Traveling to Cagliari doesn't have to break the bank. With a bit of planning, you can enjoy a full day of exploring, eating, and relaxing without spending too much. Here's a breakdown to help you set a realistic daily budget while still having a great time.

Food Costs

Cagliari offers many ways to eat well on any budget. If you're just grabbing something light, you can find fresh focaccia, pizza slices, or sandwiches for as little as **€2 to €3**. These are perfect if you're on the move or exploring during lunch. Many bakeries and local takeaways (rosticcerie) offer affordable and tasty options.

For a sit-down lunch or dinner at a mid-range restaurant, expect to pay **€12 to €18** for a pasta dish or main course. You'll find plenty of small trattorias and osterias serving Sardinian specialties like malloreddus (a type of pasta) or seafood risotto.

If you'd like to treat yourself to a more refined dinner with fresh seafood and wine, prices usually start around **€25 to €30 per person**. This would include an appetizer, a main dish, and a glass of local wine.

To save money, consider eating your main meal at lunch when some restaurants offer "menu del giorno" (daily specials) for a fixed price, usually around **€10-€15**.

Transport Costs

Cagliari has an affordable and efficient public transport system. A single ticket for the bus or metro costs **€1.30** and is valid for **90 minutes**. If you plan to travel several times in a day, it's better to get a **24-hour pass for €3.50**, which gives you unlimited travel within that time.

If you're arriving at or departing from the airport, the **shuttle bus** between **Elmas Airport and Piazza Matteotti** in the city center is also **€1.30**. It's quick and easy to use.

Taxi fares start at around **€5** and go up depending on distance and time of day. For example, a trip from the airport to the city center might cost around **€20**. Taxis are convenient, especially at night or when public transport is limited.

If you're comfortable biking, renting a **shared bike or e-scooter** is another affordable way to get around. Prices start at **€0.15-€0.30 per minute**, depending on the provider.

Attraction Costs

One of the best things about Cagliari is that **many of the top sights are free**. Walking through the historic Castello district, visiting viewpoints like the **Bastione** di Saint Remy, and entering local churches like **Cattedrale di Santa Maria** won't cost anything.

Museums are reasonably priced. The **National Archaeological Museum** is about €6, and other smaller museums range from €3 to €8. Guided tours of the **Roman Amphitheatre** or historic sites are around €7 to €10, depending on whether it's a private or group tour.

To save money, look for **combo tickets** that give you access to several museums at a reduced price. In summer, Cagliari may also offer a **"Cagliari Card"**, which includes transport and discounts for cultural sites—this is especially helpful if you plan to visit many places in a short time.

Overall Daily Budget

If you're on a **budget trip**, you can expect to spend around **€50 per day**, which covers simple meals, local transportation, and one paid attraction.

For **mid-range travelers**, planning for **€60-€70 per day** gives you room for a nice dinner, a museum visit, and maybe even a short taxi ride or gelato break.

Language Tips:

Italian is widely spoken in Cagliari, but using a few local words can really improve your experience. Even if you don't speak Italian fluently, showing a little effort helps build a connection with locals and makes interactions more pleasant.

Here are some common and useful phrases in both **Italian and Sardinian** that will come in handy.

Basic Italian Phrases

- **Buongiorno** (bwohn-jor-noh) – Good morning
  This is a friendly way to greet people in shops, cafés, and museums.

- **Grazie mille** (grah-tsee-eh mee-leh) – Thank you very much
  Saying thank you with a smile is always appreciated.

- **Per favore** (per fah-vo-reh) – Please
  Whether you're ordering food or asking for help, this word is polite and simple.

- **Un caffè, per favore** – A coffee, please
  If you're stopping at a café, this phrase will get you a classic Italian espresso.

- **Dove è...?** – Where is...?
  Useful for asking directions. For example, "Dove è la stazione?" (Where is the station?)

- **Scusi** – Excuse me
  A polite way to get someone's attention or move past someone in a crowded place.

Helpful Sardinian Words

While Italian is the main language, Sardinia has its own unique language—**Sardinian**—which locals are proud of. Even using one or two words can earn you a warm smile.

- **Comente istas?** (koh-men-teh ees-tahs) – How are you?
  This is a casual greeting among friends and locals.

- **Bona die** (boh-nah dee-eh) – Hello / Good day
  Try using this instead of "Ciao" for a more local feel.

Most people in Cagliari will understand you if you speak in basic Italian or even slow English. But showing interest in local language and culture is always seen as respectful.

Tips for Communicating

- **Speak slowly and clearly.** Many locals understand English but may not be fluent.

- **Use gestures.** Pointing or using your hands helps get the message across if you're unsure of the words.

- **Download a translation app.** Apps like Google Translate can be a lifesaver when reading menus or signs.

Even if you forget the exact phrase, don't worry. A smile and the effort to try is what people remember most.

Health and Safety Tips for Travelers

Staying healthy and safe in Cagliari is straightforward, but a little preparation goes a long way. While Cagliari is a safe and friendly city, travelers should still take basic precautions. Knowing how to handle common situations—like sun exposure, minor illnesses, or finding help—can help make your trip stress-free.

General Safety

Cagliari has a low crime rate, and violent crime is rare. Most visitors enjoy their stay without any issues. That said, **pickpocketing can happen**, especially in crowded places like the **San Benedetto Market**, on busy bus routes, and during festivals. Always keep an eye on your belongings. Avoid carrying too much cash or wearing expensive jewelry, and use a **crossbody bag or money belt** when walking around tourist areas.

At night, central areas like **Marina** and **Castello** are generally safe, but it's best to stay in well-lit, populated streets. If you're unsure about walking back to your hotel, taxis are available and reasonably priced.

Drinking Water and Food Safety

Tap water in Cagliari is safe to drink, so there's no need to buy bottled water. Locals often refill bottles at public fountains. Carrying a reusable water bottle is a good idea, especially in the summer when the heat can be intense.

Food safety is also not a concern. Restaurants, markets, and food stands maintain high hygiene standards. If you have allergies or dietary restrictions, it helps to learn a few Italian or Sardinian words (like *senza glutine* for gluten-free or *niente formaggio* for no cheese). When in doubt, ask the staff—they're usually happy to help.

Heat, Sun, and Nature Safety

Cagliari gets **very hot in summer**, especially in July and August. If you're hiking trails like the **Sella del Diavolo**, try to start early in the morning or later in the evening to avoid peak sun hours. Always wear **sunscreen**, a **hat**, and **light, breathable clothing**. Bring water with you when heading to Poetto Beach or the parks, as not all areas have easy access to cafes or shops.

If you're swimming or snorkeling, keep an eye out for jellyfish warnings posted at beaches. These are not usually dangerous but can be painful. Local lifeguards or beach bars often share updates about conditions.

Pharmacies and Medical Help

For minor health issues like headaches, allergies, or stomach trouble, **pharmacies (Farmacia)** are your first stop. They are easy to find—just look for the green cross sign. Most pharmacists speak basic English and can recommend over-the-counter remedies. Common items like pain relievers, cold medicine, and even motion sickness pills are available without a prescription.

If you need to see a doctor for something more serious, there are public clinics and private practices available. **Ospedale Brotzu** is the largest hospital in the area and is well-equipped for emergencies. It's accessible via **Bus Line 5**, and staff there are used to assisting tourists.

Emergency Numbers

In case of emergencies, **dial 112**, the EU-wide number for police, ambulance, or fire services. This number connects you to a multilingual operator and is free from any phone. You can also visit the nearest hospital emergency room (**"Pronto Soccorso"**) for urgent care.

Internet, SIM Cards, and Staying Connected

Staying connected in Cagliari is easy and affordable. Whether you want to check directions, post photos, or stay in touch with friends and family, there are plenty of ways to stay online during your trip.

Free Wi-Fi and Public Access

Many hotels, cafés, restaurants, and some public spaces in Cagliari offer **free Wi-Fi**. In central areas like **Piazza Yenne**, **Via Roma**, and **Bastione di Saint Remy**, you'll often find signs advertising free or password-protected Wi-Fi for customers. Wi-Fi quality can vary, so don't rely on it for heavy use like video calls unless you're in a hotel with strong service.

If you need guaranteed access for work or travel planning, consider getting a local SIM card or portable hotspot.

Buying a SIM Card in Cagliari

A **prepaid Italian SIM card** is one of the best ways to stay connected. You can buy one at the airport, at mobile stores in the city, or even at some tobacco shops. Major providers include:

- **TIM**
- **Vodafone**
- **WindTre**

These companies offer **tourist plans** with 10–20 GB of data, local minutes, and some international calls for around **€15–€25**, valid for **30 days**. Be sure to bring your **passport**, as registration is required. Setup usually takes 5–10 minutes, and staff can help insert and activate your SIM.

If your phone is **unlocked**, switching SIMs is simple. If not, you may want to look into using an **eSIM**.

eSIM and Online Options

If your smartphone supports **eSIM**, you can purchase a data plan **online before your trip**. This option allows you to skip the store visit entirely—just scan a QR code, install the plan, and you're ready to go. Companies like **Airalo** or **Holafly** offer Italy-specific packages.

This is a good choice if you're arriving late or just want a quick setup without handling physical SIM cards.

Other Connectivity Tips

- **Bring a power bank**: Exploring the city, taking photos, and using maps can drain your phone battery fast. A small portable charger can save the day, especially on long outings or beach days.
- **Use offline maps**: Download offline versions of Cagliari in apps like Google Maps or Maps.me. This helps in areas with weak signal or when trying to save data.
- **Turn off background data**: To make your data last longer, adjust your phone settings to stop apps from using data in the background.

Accessibility and Traveling with Kids or Seniors

Preparing for an Easy Trip

Cagliari's old streets and historic sites look lovely, but cobblestones and stairs can slow you down. A little planning goes a long way. Before you pack, think about how everyone in your group moves around. Check routes, book transport in advance, and scope out rest stops so that kids stay happy and seniors stay comfortable.

Mobility

Getting around by public transit can be straightforward if you know which lines to choose. Bus line 1 and many of the newer CTM buses have low floors and ramps, so wheelchairs and walkers roll on easily. You can buy tickets at kiosks or via the "Muver" app—just remember to validate your ticket on board.

The city's single light-rail line is fully step-free, with elevators at every station, including the stop at Piazza Repubblica. From there, you can reach the airport or connect to buses. If you need extra help, you can call CTM customer service (phone number on their website) at least 24 hours ahead to request assistance boarding or on-board.

Traveling with Kids

Cagliari really shines for families. Many of its wide piazzas have small playgrounds where little ones can burn off energy between sightseeing stops. Parco di Monte Urpinu is a top pick: it has shaded paths, a small café with snacks, and even a fish pond that kids love to visit.

Keep children happy by breaking up museum visits with gelato by the sea—there are gelaterias every few blocks along the Marina. Pack a lightweight stroller with good wheels for gravel or cobblestones; it'll help you move faster and avoid tired legs. A foldable rain cover can also protect them if a summer shower pops up.

Traveling with Seniors

For older travelers, taxis offer a comfortable way to avoid steep hills and crowded buses. Fares are regulated, and a ride within the city center usually costs €8–€12. In high season, call to reserve a wheelchair-accessible cab or book via a taxi-app early in the day.

When planning museum trips, visit websites ahead of time to confirm elevator access and restroom locations. The Archaeological Museum and Museo del Risorgimento both have lifts. If someone in your group finds long walks tiring, plan for shorter outings—perhaps a morning at Bastione di Saint Remy followed by lunch at a ground-floor café.

Chapter 11: Suggested Itineraries for Every Type of Traveler

Cagliari in One Day:

If you're short on time but still want a strong feel for Cagliari, this one-day itinerary covers the city's heart, taste, coast, and charm. It's ideal for cruise stopovers, layovers, or travelers passing through. The day moves at a relaxed pace, starting from the old city center and ending by the sea, with views that are worth every step.

Morning: Explore Castello District (9:00 AM – 11:00 AM)

Begin your day in **Castello**, the oldest and most historic part of Cagliari. The district is located on a hill, so wear comfortable shoes for the cobbled streets and gentle slopes. Head to **Piazza Palazzo** (09124 Cagliari), where your walk begins.

Wander through the medieval alleys toward **Torre dell'Elefante** (Via Santa Croce) and **Torre di San Pancrazio**, both of which are open to the public for a small fee (entry is often free or €2–€3 during off-season promotions). These towers offer panoramic views over the city and are great for photos.

As you walk along **Via Santa Croce**, you'll find small, family-run cafés. I stopped at one for a quick espresso (€1.20), and the warm welcome from the barista made me feel instantly at home. It's a good moment to pause, sip slowly, and enjoy the relaxed rhythm of local life.

Midday: Local Flavors at San Benedetto Market (12:00 PM – 1:30 PM)

Walk down **Via del Fossario** and catch a local bus (Line 1 or M) to **San Benedetto Market** (Piazza Mercato, 09122 Cagliari). A single ticket costs €1.30 and can be purchased at any newsstand or tabacchi (tobacco shop). The ride takes around 15 minutes.

This two-level market is one of Italy's largest and liveliest indoor food markets. On the ground floor, you'll find fresh seafood, meats, and cheeses. Upstairs, there's a wide range of fruits, vegetables, and baked goods. For about €5, you can pick up a small tasting spread: **pane carasau** (crispy flatbread), **pecorino cheese**, and a sweet fig jam.

This is a great place to interact with locals and try small bites without committing to a full sit-down lunch.

Afternoon: Poetto Beach Walk (2:00 PM – 5:30 PM)

After your market snack, head to **Poetto Beach**. From the market, walk to Viale Regina Margherita and take **Bus Line PQ or PF**. It's about a 20-minute ride to the beach area. Buses run frequently throughout the day.

Poetto stretches over 8 kilometers and is ideal for a relaxed walk. You'll see joggers, families, and fishermen all enjoying the long shoreline. You can stop at **Marina Piccola**, rent a sunbed (€5–€10), or just sit along the pier with a gelato (€2.50) from one of the kiosks.

Evening: Sunset at Bastione di Saint Remy (6:00 PM – 7:30 PM)

Head back toward the city center and climb to the **Bastione di Saint Remy** (Via Giuseppe Garibaldi, 09124). It's one of the best places in the city to watch the sunset—and it's completely free. From here, you'll see the rooftops glow orange as the sun dips behind the Gulf of Angels.

It's the perfect way to end your one-day adventure in Cagliari: simple, scenic, and full of local color.

A Perfect Weekend:

If you're only in Cagliari for the weekend, don't worry—you can still experience a rich mix of the city's history, food, and seaside beauty. This two-day itinerary helps you enjoy both sides of the city: the cultural heart and the coastal edge.

Day 1 – Culture & City Flavors

Start your day at the National Archaeological Museum, located at **Via Santa Croce 67, 09124 Cagliari**. The museum opens around **9 AM**, and entrance costs

€6. It's easy to get there by walking from Piazza Yenne or taking a short taxi ride if you're staying farther out. The museum holds a wide range of prehistoric, Punic, and Roman artifacts that help you understand Sardinia's deep past. One of the highlights is the collection of small bronze figures called *bronzetti*—each one tells a story. I still remember how the sunlight hit the statues just right, casting long shadows across the marble floors.

By lunchtime, walk down toward the Marina district and stop at **Trattoria Sa Domu Sarda (Via Sardegna 15)**. It's a cozy, family-run spot known for traditional Sardinian dishes. A full meal here, including porceddu (roast suckling pig) and side dishes, will cost about **€18**. If you're adventurous, try *malloreddus*, a type of Sardinian gnocchi served with sausage ragù. They're filling and flavorful.

In the afternoon, take a calm walk to the **Botanical Garden** at **Via Sant'Ignazio da Laconi, 09123 Cagliari**. Entry costs just **€3**. This garden isn't huge, but it's peaceful and shaded—perfect for a warm afternoon. You'll find exotic plants, Roman ruins, and quiet corners where you can sit and relax. There are benches throughout, so take your time and enjoy the slower pace.

As the sun begins to set, make your way to **Caffè Libarium Nostrum** at **Via Santa Croce 33** (also accessible from **Via Sardegna** if you're in the Marina). It's one of the best spots in the city for a relaxed **aperitivo**. For around **€12**, you can enjoy a small plate of local tapas (cheese, olives, cured meats) along with a chilled glass of **Vermentino**, a popular white wine in Sardinia. The view from their terrace is worth it alone—you'll see rooftops stretching out to the sea. It's a great way to close your first day.

Day 2 – Beach & Boat

Day two is all about relaxing by the water, with a mix of beach time and a scenic boat trip.

Catch **bus number 13** from **Piazza Matteotti** to **Calamosca Beach**. A one-way ticket costs **€1.30** and the ride takes around 20 minutes. Calamosca is smaller and quieter than Poetto Beach, and it's a favorite among locals. The water is calm and clear—ideal for swimming or just floating. On-site vendors rent **snorkeling gear for around €8 per hour**. The rocky seabed makes snorkeling interesting; you'll likely spot sea urchins, fish, and small crabs.

After a few hours at the beach, head to **Porticciolo della Fossa**, about a 10-minute walk from Calamosca, for a **late afternoon boat tour**. These small-group cruises typically leave around **4 PM** and last about **two hours**. You can book them in advance or ask around at the marina (average cost: **€30 per person**). Some boats offer snacks and drinks on board. Keep an eye out for **dolphins**, especially during sunset—sightings are common along this part of the Sardinian coast.

As the sun sets over the Gulf of Angels, you'll end your weekend with views that are hard to forget.

5-Day Itinerary:

This 5-day plan is ideal for travelers who want to see both sides of Cagliari—the rich culture and the beautiful coastline. It combines historical sights, nature exploration, and beach relaxation. This itinerary also includes affordable transport options, day trips, and tips to help you enjoy Cagliari at a comfortable pace.

Day 1: One-Day Historic Core

Start your trip by diving into the heart of Cagliari. Follow the full-day plan from the "One-Day Historic Core" itinerary (Chapter 11, Subheading 1). This includes visiting the **Castello District**, exploring landmarks like **Torre dell'Elefante**, the **Cattedrale di Santa Maria**, and enjoying the sunset from **Bastione di Saint Remy**. You'll walk through narrow streets, take in city views, and learn about Cagliari's past—all within walking distance. Pack water, wear comfortable shoes, and grab lunch at a local café (budget around €10–15).

Day 2: Nora Ruins & Pula Beach

This day takes you south of the city for history and sea views. Start by **renting a car** from a local agency on **Via dei Giudicati 66** (roughly €50/day). From Cagliari, drive about **40–45 minutes** to reach **Nora Archaeological Site** in Pula. There's a small parking area near the entrance. Entry to the site is **€8**, and you'll need **about 1.5 hours** to explore the Roman ruins, mosaics, and amphitheater. A guided tour adds more context, often included in the ticket price.

Afterward, head to **Pula Beach**, just a few minutes away. Bring swimwear, a towel, and sunscreen. It's a great spot to cool off and enjoy the turquoise water. For lunch, visit **Sa Cardiga e Su Pisci** (Address: SS195 km 30, Pula), a well-known seafood restaurant with outdoor seating. Expect to pay around **€20–25 per person** for a meal. Drive back to Cagliari in the late afternoon.

Day 3: Molentargius Natural Park

Today is slower-paced and focused on nature. Take **Bus Line 3** from **Piazza Matteotti** to the **Stagno entrance** of **Molentargius Natural Park**. The ride takes about **30 minutes** and costs **€1.30** (purchase ticket at a tabacchi shop or kiosk). The park is free to enter and is famous for its flamingos, wetland ecosystems, and salt pans.

Bring **binoculars** if you have them, or rent at the park's info center (availability may vary). There are well-marked walking and cycling paths. The **flamingo viewing areas** are best early in the morning or late afternoon. There's a small snack kiosk near the park's central area, but you can also pack lunch. Expect to spend **2–3 hours** exploring before heading back to the city.

Day 4: Barumini's Su Nuraxi (UNESCO Site)

This day trip takes you to one of Sardinia's most important archaeological sites. Catch a **train from Cagliari Centrale** station to **Barumini**, with a **ticket price of around €4 each way**. The journey takes about **1 hour and 20 minutes**. From Barumini station, it's a **short taxi ride** or a **20-minute walk** to **Su Nuraxi**.

Entry to the site costs **€12**, and guided tours are offered every hour. Su Nuraxi is a **3,000-year-old nuraghe**—a unique stone structure built by Sardinia's ancient civilization. Walking through its corridors and central tower gives you a direct look into prehistoric life. Bring water, wear a hat, and plan to return to Cagliari in the late afternoon.

Day 5: Leisure Day at Tuerredda Beach

Wrap up your trip with a relaxing beach day. Catch a **bus from Largo Carlo Felice** (in central Cagliari) to **Chia**. Tickets cost about **€4 return**, and buses leave several times a day. From Chia, take a **small ferry or taxi boat (€5)** to reach the stunning **Tuerredda Beach**.

Tuerredda is known for its **clear water and calm waves**, perfect for swimming and sunbathing. You can rent a beach chair and umbrella for around €15 for the day. There's a beach bar where you can grab sandwiches and cold drinks (budget €10–15). You'll want to stay here until late afternoon before catching your return bus to Cagliari.

7-Day Deep Dive:

If you have a full week to explore Cagliari, this itinerary gives you a balanced mix of city sights, natural beauty, nearby villages, and relaxing moments by the sea. It's great for travelers who want to go beyond the basics and experience Cagliari at a slower, deeper pace. You'll walk through local neighborhoods, take scenic day trips, and enjoy both beaches and mountain parks without rushing.

Days 1–2: Follow the 5-Day Itinerary Plan

To get started, spend your first two days following the 5-day plan. This includes visiting Cagliari's Castello district, the National Archaeological Museum, San Benedetto Market, Poetto Beach, Molentargius Park, and possibly a trip to Nora or Barumini. This part gives you a solid foundation of the city's history, food, and coastline.

Day 3: Explore Villanova Neighborhood on Foot

Villanova is one of Cagliari's most charming and less crowded neighborhoods. It's a great area to explore on foot. Begin your morning with a coffee at **Caffè Flavio** (Via Santa Croce 23). A cappuccino here costs about €1.50, and the atmosphere is cozy and local.

From there, take a slow walk through the colorful streets filled with plants, murals, and small artisan shops. Make your way toward **Via Sassari**, where you'll find several street art pieces painted on building walls and shutters. Many of these works tell stories about local life or culture. It's a peaceful part of the city where you can take photos, chat with locals, or simply enjoy the quiet.

Day 4: Monte Urpinu Park and Picnic

Monte Urpinu is a green hill close to the center of Cagliari. Take **Metro C** and get off at the "Monte Urpinu" stop. Entry to the park is free. It's a perfect spot for a picnic, reading a book, or just relaxing under pine trees with a view of the city and sea.

Pack a light lunch (around €6) from a local bakery—maybe some focaccia, cheese, and fruit—and enjoy it at one of the picnic tables. You may spot peacocks, ducks, and turtles around the small pond. The park is safe and family-friendly, and you can easily spend 2-3 hours here.

Day 5: Day Trip to Iglesias

Take a train from **Cagliari Centrale Station** to **Iglesias** (ticket costs about €7 each way; the ride takes around 1 hour and 15 minutes). Iglesias is a historic town in southwestern Sardinia known for its mining past and Gothic architecture.

Visit the **Mining Art Museum** (Via Roma 47; entry €5), where you'll learn about the region's deep mining roots and see tools, maps, and photographs from past centuries. Then walk to the **Cathedral of Santa Chiara**, a peaceful Gothic church in the center of town. Enjoy lunch in one of the small piazzas nearby—many places offer local dishes like malloreddus (Sardinian gnocchi) for under €15.

Days 6-7: Back in Cagliari – Beach and Farewell

On your final two days, take it easy and enjoy Cagliari's relaxing side. Head back to **Poetto Beach**—you can rent a sunbed for around €10 or just walk along the shore with a gelato (€2.50). If you're up for something active, rent a bike and ride the paved path along the coast.

For sunset, return to **Bastione di Saint Remy** for a sweeping view over the Gulf of Angels. It's one of the best spots in the city to say goodbye.

End your trip with dinner at **Il Labirinto** (Via Sardegna 35). The seafood here is fresh, and the service is friendly. A full dinner with wine costs around €25 per person. Try the fregola with clams or grilled calamari—both are local favorites.

Cagliari for Families:

Cagliari is a great destination for families. It offers a mix of fun, education, and open spaces where kids can play and explore safely. The city is easy to walk around, and many attractions are close together. Whether your children love animals, playgrounds, sea life, or sweet treats, this itinerary gives you a full day of enjoyment for all ages.

Morning: Museo del Cavallino Marino – A Playful Start to the Day

Begin your family day at the **Museo del Cavallino Marino** (Sea Horse Museum), located at **Via dei Tribunali 10**. Entry costs **€4 for kids and €6 for adults**, and the museum is open from 9:30 AM to 1 PM. This small but charming museum is designed with children in mind. It focuses on marine animals and the local ecosystem in a way that's easy to understand.

Kids can enjoy hands-on exhibits—touching real shells, using magnifying glasses, and watching short videos about sea creatures. My niece, who's six, was fascinated by the miniature models of sea horses and kept pressing buttons that made fish sounds. Staff are friendly and speak some English, which helps if your Italian is limited.

To get there, take **bus line M** or walk from the city center (15–20 minutes uphill if walking). There's a baby-changing area and restroom on-site.

Midday: Picnic and Play at Parco di Monte Claro

After the museum, take a short taxi ride or bus number 9 or 20 to **Parco di Monte Claro** (Via Is Mirrionis). Entry is **free**, and it's one of the best parks in Cagliari for kids. There's a large, well-equipped **playground**, open grassy areas for running around, and shaded benches under pine trees—perfect for a picnic.

Bring snacks or pick up sandwiches and fruit from a nearby supermarket. There's a pond with ducks, a small fountain, and even an area for teens to play basketball. Parents can relax while kids explore. The park is stroller-friendly with paved paths, and there's usually a vendor nearby selling ice cream or cold drinks.

Spend about 1–2 hours here, especially if your kids need a break from structured activities.

Afternoon: Aquarium Cala Fighera – Sea Life Up Close

From the park, head toward **Aquarium Cala Fighera** at **Strada Cala Fighera**. Entry is around **€15 per person**, which includes a **shuttle bus** from the city center (departures from Piazza Matteotti). The aquarium is small but interactive, perfect for younger children who may get tired quickly in larger aquariums.

What makes this place special is that kids are allowed to **touch starfish**, sea cucumbers, and other soft marine creatures under the guidance of staff. There are colorful tanks filled with local fish, and the guides do a great job explaining their habitat in simple language. The entire visit takes about 1–1.5 hours.

This was a highlight for my nephew, who was amazed by the "dancing octopus" in one tank. There's also a small café outside the aquarium if you need refreshments.

Evening: Gelato Crawl on Via Roma

Wrap up the day with a fun and tasty **gelato crawl along Via Roma**. This waterfront street has several top-rated **gelaterias**, all within walking distance. Plan to visit 2–3 spots and let your kids pick a scoop from each. Most places charge around **€2 per scoop**.

Popular stops include **Gelateria Peter Pan**, **Vanilla Creams & Fruits**, and **Antico Caffè**. Choose flavors like Nutella, strawberry, pistachio, or even lemon basil if you want something more local.

This is a simple, low-cost way to end the day on a happy note. Parents can grab a coffee or even a glass of wine while kids enjoy their ice cream. The promenade along Via Roma is wide, flat, and perfect for an after-dinner stroll before heading back to your hotel.

Cagliari for Food Lovers:

If you enjoy discovering a place through its food, Cagliari won't disappoint. Sardinian cuisine is full of bold flavors, fresh seafood, traditional pastries, and excellent wines. This itinerary is designed for travelers who love to eat their way through a city. From markets and bakeries to fine dining and local wine bars, this food-focused route covers it all—complete with real-life tips, prices, and locations.

Start the Day with a Traditional Pastry

Begin your morning at **Pasticceria Cocco**, a popular pastry shop located at *Via Regina Margherita 21*, near the city center. This bakery is known for its **seadas**—a typical Sardinian dessert made from fried dough, filled with soft cheese, and drizzled with honey. It's usually eaten after meals, but locals don't mind enjoying it for breakfast either. Expect to pay about **€4** for one serving. The pastry is sweet but not overly sugary, with a satisfying mix of crispy and creamy textures. It's best enjoyed with a strong Italian espresso, which you can get at the counter for **around €1.20**.

Explore the San Benedetto Market with a Local Guide

Next, head to **Mercato di San Benedetto**, located at *Via Francesco Cocco Ortu 50*. It's about a 15-minute walk or a quick bus ride from the city center. This is the **largest indoor market in Cagliari**, and one of the largest in all of Italy. It opens early in the morning, but the best time to go for a guided tour is around **10:00 AM**, when the place is buzzing but not overcrowded.

You can book a **market tour with a local guide** for approximately **€25 per person**. This includes several tastings—expect to sample **bottarga** (cured fish roe), **pecorino cheese**, **Sardinian olives**, and seasonal fruits. A good guide will also explain the stories behind the products and point you to the best stalls if you want to shop on your own later. Don't forget to try some **local olive oil**, usually served with thin slices of bread.

Lunch at One of Cagliari's Best Restaurants

For lunch, treat yourself to a fine dining experience at **Dal Corsaro**, a Michelin-starred restaurant located at *Via Sassari 58*. The restaurant offers a **tasting menu for about €65 per person**, which may sound pricey, but the quality and presentation make it worth it—especially for food lovers. When I visited, the meal included a local **sea bass served with wild herbs**, and a glass of **Cannonau**, a full-bodied red wine that's native to Sardinia. The staff are friendly, and they're happy to explain each course, which adds to the overall experience. Make sure to **book in advance**, especially during the weekend.

Evening Wine Bar Hopping in the Marina District

As the sun sets, head to the **Marina District** near *Via Roma*. This lively area is filled with **wine bars**, each offering a different selection of Sardinian and Italian wines. Many bars offer a small **aperitivo**—a glass of wine served with **cheese, breadsticks, or olives**. Each stop will cost around **€8 per glass with a small plate**. I recommend **Vineria Tzè**, a cozy spot with a relaxed vibe and a well-curated wine list. Another good choice is **Fico Wine Bar**, which sometimes hosts live acoustic music.

This relaxed wine-tasting crawl is a great way to end your food-filled day. You'll also likely meet locals and other travelers, making it a social and satisfying experience.

Adventure & Nature Itinerary:

If you're someone who enjoys staying active while traveling, Cagliari offers plenty of outdoor experiences that combine nature, beautiful views, and a bit of a workout. Whether you're hiking along cliffs, paddling through the sea, or biking through city parks, this 3-day adventure itinerary will help you discover the wilder side of Cagliari.

Day 1: Hike the Sella del Diavolo Trail

This hike is one of the best ways to see Cagliari from above and enjoy coastal views without leaving the city. It's a great way to kick off your trip with movement and scenery.

Details:

Start your day early and head to **Viale Calamosca**, which leads to the **Sella del Diavolo trailhead**. The trail is free to access and takes about 1.5 to 2 hours roundtrip, depending on your pace. The path is mostly dirt and rocks, so wear sturdy shoes and bring a bottle of water and a snack (about €5 total if bought in advance from a nearby shop).

Along the trail, you'll pass pine trees, rocky cliffs, and stunning views of **Poetto Beach** and **Golfo degli Angeli** (Gulf of Angels). At the top, the **Saracen Tower** stands as a reminder of the area's medieval past, and it makes for an excellent photo stop. It's not uncommon to see locals jogging here in the morning. I met a friendly local who gave me a tip about the best rock to sit on for watching the sunset – I returned the next day just to try it.

How to Get There:
Take bus PF or PQ from **Piazza Matteotti** to **Viale Calamosca**. The ride takes about 20 minutes and costs €1.30 each way.

Day 2: Sea Kayaking from Marina Piccola

For a different view of Cagliari, get on the water. A kayaking trip offers not just exercise, but also a chance to explore hidden coves and marine life.

Details:
Book a **2-hour guided sea kayak tour** (about €50 per person) from **Marina Piccola**, located at the end of **Lungomare Poetto**. Most tours include safety gear and a quick training session, so beginners are welcome.

You'll paddle along the rocky coastline toward hidden grottos and quiet coves. There's often time to stop and swim or snorkel in calm waters. One guide told me stories about smugglers who once used the caves along this route.

How to Get There:
Take bus PQ to **Marina Piccola** or walk along Poetto Beach if you're nearby. The marina is clearly marked and easy to find.

Day 3: Mountain Biking and Beach Cool Down

End your active itinerary with a day of cycling through one of Cagliari's best green spaces, followed by a relaxing swim at a quiet beach.

Details:
Rent a mountain bike from **Monte Urpinu Bike Center** at **Piazza Giovanni XXIII** (around €20 for a full day). From here, head into **Monte Urpinu Park**, a peaceful green space with hilly trails and great city views. It's a fun way to explore without dealing with traffic.

After cycling through the park, follow the bike path toward **Calamosca Beach**. It's smaller than Poetto but less crowded, making it a great place to relax and cool off. The beach is free and there's usually a vendor nearby selling cold drinks and sandwiches.

How to Get There:
Bike from the rental shop directly to Monte Urpinu, then to **Via Calamosca**. You can also return the bike and take bus 5 to **Calamosca**.

Conclusion

As our journey through Cagliari draws to a close, you've seen how this sun-soaked port city is more than a stopover—it's a place that lingers in your memory long after you've left. From wandering ancient alleyways in the Castello district to sinking your toes into the soft sand of Poetto Beach, Cagliari offers genuine moments that invite you to slow down, breathe deeply, and savor life at Mediterranean pace.

Remember, the real magic happens when you stray off the beaten path. That hidden cove at Calamosca or the quiet streets of Villanova aren't just photo ops—they're snapshots of everyday Sardinian life. Strike up a conversation with a local at San Benedetto Market, and you'll discover why fresh bottarga or a glass of Cannonau wine tastes so much better when shared with new friends. These personal connections are what turn a trip into a true adventure.

Practical note: don't try to pack it all into one day. Choose three or four "must-see" sights—maybe the Roman Amphitheatre, Bastione di Saint Remy, and a relaxed afternoon at Molentargius Natural Park—and build your days around them. Leave space in your schedule for a late-morning espresso on a shady café terrace or an unplanned detour to chase a sunset over the Gulf of Angels. That flexibility is key to feeling at home in Cagliari rather than just checking boxes off a list.

As you plan, think about timing—Cagliari's summer heat can be intense, so mornings and evenings are prime for exploring. If you visit in spring or fall, you'll enjoy cooler walks up Sella del Diavolo and quieter beaches. And pack layers: sea breezes can turn chilly once the sun dips. Finally, embrace simplicity: a good pair of walking shoes, a reusable water bottle, and a sense of curiosity will carry you farther than any fancy gear.

Above all, let Cagliari surprise you. Follow your instincts—whether that means sampling a new street-food stall or veering down a narrow side street—to create stories you'll want to tell back home. By the time you leave, this lively city won't just be another dot on the map; it'll feel like a close friend who welcomed you with open arms and taught you a little Sardinian warmth along the way.

Safe travels, and may your memories of Cagliari be as bright and lasting as the Sardinian sun.

Printed in Dunstable, United Kingdom